'In *A Re-mapping of Womanhood and Creativity: A Literary and Depth Psychological Perspective*, Clara Oropeza explores the profound impact of mother-daughter relationships on our personal and creative lives. Oropeza illuminates how our mothers, both biological and literary, empower us to claim our place as artists in the world. This book is sure to spark important conversations about the unique challenges and opportunities faced by women of color in claiming our creative power and healing the mother wound.'

Reyna Grande, *author of* The Distance Between Us

'Join Dr. Oropeza in *A Re-mapping of Womanhood and Creativity* on a scholarly and deeply personal journey as she explores the complex relationships between mothers and daughters, creativity, and identity. This book offers a fresh perspective on the ways in which women can re-map their lives, challenging patriarchal norms, and reclaim their feminine gaze. This book is a must-read for scholars and individuals interested in feminist theory, depth psychology, and literary studies, as well as anyone looking to explore the transformative power of maternal relationships.'

Nora Strejilevich, PhD, *author of* A Single Numberless Death

'*A Re-mapping of Womanhood and Creativity* examines the lives of multicultural women across generations. Oropeza taps into her personal experiences to access her matrilinear legacy and a deep connection into how it inspires her creativity. Oropeza contributes a fascinating psychological analysis of Anaïs Nin's creativity, voice, and feminine imagery as she dives into the formative relationship between Nin and her mother. This book is important as it comes to fruition at a key moment in history, when the lives of women are evermore threatened by a patriarchal order attempting to gain control.'

Sylvie Eve Blum-Reid, PhD, *University of Florida, editor of* Impressions from Paris: Women Creatives in Interwar Years France

A Re-mapping of Womanhood and Creativity

A Re-mapping of Womanhood and Creativity investigates the diverse ways in which women set out to find a matrilineal line as a wellspring for creative transformation, and, through a lens of analytical psychology, how we read women's literary history and narratives about womanhood.

While following the feminine influences that forged her own search and nature as a writer, this book re-maps the life and work of Clara Oropeza's literary mother, Anaïs Nin, focusing on Nin's formative affinity with her mother, alongside her own personal mother. In this mother-map, Oropeza looks closely at the relationship between mothers and daughters, the formation of the maternal wound, and ways to move towards healing. Oropeza examines the pivotal role that a reconnection to a maternal line has in shaping a woman's creative life. This book argues that synthesizing our intellectual, spiritual and ancestral ways of knowing, away from the harmful narratives that shape our lives, is essential today. With scholarly and personal insight, Oropeza sheds new light on how women come to shores of understanding themselves beyond unresolved familial and historical tensions.

Combining literature, myth and psychology, this book will be an illuminating read for students, scholars and professionals in the areas of literature, psychoanalysis and mythology. This book will be crucial reading for women, in particular women of color, interested in the process of individuation, creativity and womanhood.

Clara Oropeza, PhD, is a Professor of English Composition and Literature at Santa Barbara City College. Her research combines literary studies, comparative mythology, feminist and cultural theory, and depth psychology. She is the author of *Anaïs Nin: A Myth of Her Own* and various essays. She received her BA and MA in English Literature from California State University, Los Angeles, and her PhD in Comparative Mythology and Literature with an emphasis in Depth Psychology from Pacifica Graduate Institute.

A Re-mapping of Womanhood and Creativity

A Literary and Depth Psychological Perspective

Clara Oropeza, PhD

Routledge
Taylor & Francis Group

LONDON AND NEW YORK

Designed cover image: Mary By Erika Carter

First published 2025
by Routledge
4 Park Square, Milton Park, Abingdon, Oxon OX14 4RN

and by Routledge
605 Third Avenue, New York, NY 10158

Routledge is an imprint of the Taylor & Francis Group, an informa business

British Library Cataloguing-in-Publication Data
A catalogue record for this book is available from the British Library

ISBN: 978-1-032-18712-9 (hbk)
ISBN: 978-1-032-18711-2 (pbk)
ISBN: 978-1-003-25585-7 (ebk)

DOI: 10.4324/9781003255857

Typeset in Times New Roman
by Taylor & Francis Books

Para mis antipasadas. And for my mother, with love.

Contents

Figures

Acknowledgements

I thank Mark Wanek, my husband, for his boundless love, wisdom and support. For his companionship and emotional support on research trips, and literary residencies in Paris, I am grateful beyond words. For my sisters, Ana Oropeza-Parra, Hilda-Shraddha Oropeza, Elvia Rodriguez, and Thelma Ruiz, with whom I share a rich matrilineal heritage. For Criselda Rodriguez and Vicente Rodriguez: may they grow up honoring the strength of their matrilineal lineage and knowing the power of their own stories.

Thank you to my *querida* friends, sisters in arms, who discussed, read, edited and encouraged me, especially Dolores Rivera, I. Murphy Lewis, Sylvie Eve Blum-Reid and Nora Strejilevich. I am lucky to have their deep friendship.

A special thank you to Cheryle Van Scoy for her healing insights, and for sharing the intimate details of her profound experience with Anaïs Nin during Nin's final moments on earth, as I write about in Chapter 2.

Thank you to Erika Carter for generously allowing me to use her beautiful painting *Mary* for my book cover. Erika's acts of kindness in our community and in my life deeply inspire me.

Para mi mama, aprecio su disposición para compartir la historia de su vida y por confiar en mí para escribirla. Sus ideas conducen a avances no sólo en este libro, sino también en mi vida.

To all the literary mothers who informed the ideas in this book and beyond.

I am grateful to Tree Wright from Anaïs Nin's literary estate for allowing me to quote from the archival material, as I reference in Chapter 2. For the use of Gloria Anzaldúa's epigraph from *Borderlands/La Frontera: The New Mestiza*, featured in the Preface, I thank Joan Pinkvoss from Aunt Lute Books.

Finally, I thank my students whose love of literature inspires and nourishes me.

Preface

Lay of the Land: A Mother-Map

> My Chicana identity is grounded in the Indian woman's history of resistance.
> Gloria Anzaldúa (*Borderlands* 43)

Using elements such as details, names and symbols, maps hold the power to shape visibility and consciousness, and to reveal relationships. My search for women in history, literary and familial, has compelled me to take up the cartographer's impulse: to orient by way of mapping places and creations, of demarcating to fill in the gaps of my knowledge of women's voices, feminine imagination and instincts, and their histories of resistance. The kind of geography that I am interested in is of both uncharted and charted lands, crossings, and streams of stories that exist in the inner chambers of the self, awaiting discovery. Maps invite contemplation of relationships across landscapes, boundaries, social and cultural spheres, between the past and present. I am intrigued by the interior and exterior topographies (psychic places and physical locations) where womanhood stakes claim in various historical times across myriad landscapes. I am drawn to places where personal history meets cultural history. This map, *A Re-mapping of Womanhood and Creativity: A Literary and Depth Psychological Perspective*, examines the lives of multicultural women of multi-generations who have created a place of their own while seeking freedom and orientation in life.

Patriarchy is composed of the social systems that place women in psychological and physical subordination to men, as men hold the positions of power and privilege. It has mapped womanhood across generations and cultures. The patriarchal world we live in has plotted the lives of women into the margins of its society. Maps themselves can promote the visibility of people and places, but maps can also foster invisibility. For instance, Western cartography has its foundation in colonization, as it was used to identify lands to claim underserved ownership. Cartography was also used to impose a Eurocentric view, a singular way of relating to the world, according to the way the colonizer mapped the standards for the world. Through maps, viewpoints and stories, the gender norms of the masculine were drawn up as rational, clever, ordered and good. Matrilineal legacies, on the other hand, were distorted, deeming the feminine as irrational, threatening, weak, and a chaotic force to be disconnected from or feared. In the Western creation myths, we see disturbing themes of the patriarchy usurping a mother's birth-giving power (Eve born of Adam's rib and Athena from Zeus's head). Those maps have also silenced women from the historical archives (women's achievements overshadowed in scholarship). Our mother's stories have, too often, been relegated to narratives of shame by our fathers and society. Even in today's twenty-first century in the United States, women's bodies remain in control by laws written by white men (*Roe v. Wade* reversal in the United States in 2022). Resistance is just as important now as it has been in the past.

In a patriarchal-ordered world, women's bodies have been oriented towards spheres that limit, if not crush, our autonomy. Women have inherited the psychological impacts of the expectations to nurture children and men (the male artist as creator) at the expense of her own creative will. Women are made to feel like trespassers of our own imagination as our experiences continue to be filtered through masculine products, such as through art. Although our matrilineal legacy is our inherited right from which to draw feminine gifts and inspiration, it has often been obstructed, or in some cases stripped from our personal and cultural histories. My own experience of not having clear access or intimate knowledge of my matrilineal legacy, a feminine wellspring from which to draw creative strength, is what motivated me to write this book. Seen this way, this is the book that I have needed to read.

The world has long needed to restore this ancient imbalance and question the perspectives, gaps and fissures of the colonizers' consciousness and unconsciousness. Our ancestors, scholars, and artists have already been reorienting themselves through the process of restructuring the narratives that have limited their well-being, altering our view of the potential for women to individuate. Through the brave and pioneering work of many of our female forbearers, women have been exposing what has been excluded. They have testified to other ways of being, knowing, and experiencing the world. However, the urgent need still exists to re-map what we know and how we have come to know it, including what has previously been unacknowledged in our personal histories.

There is a process for rewriting ourselves out of places where representations of womanhood have been distorted. As this process evolves, for many of us, the need to re-map ourselves into the landscapes, both inner and outer, is vital so we can flourish. The initial stage of the process identifies how we become conscious of the harmful structures and narratives that occupy our imagination and our psychology. It is this experience that I am most interested in mapping throughout this book. Here, I survey what it means to pursue a yearning toward filling the void of female inheritance, histories, and legacies, in both literary and personal terms. In essence, this is a mother-map where I explore how the formative role of searching for the feminine plays within the individuation path of the women whose lives I write about. I argue that mapping a matrilineal lineage can be a feminine creative source from which to ground our search for freedom. Some of the questions I dwell on are: how does a desire to honor a feminine lineage coincide with the quest to live a deeper sense of one's own feminine voice and creativity? How does tending the maternal wound, including the shame and grief stemming from the abuse of the feminine, position us for healing in our lives and in our communities? To what extent is the process of creating a language (spiritual, literary, symbolic), a path towards gaining an inner feminine authority that helps us resist the challenges we face as women, especially as women of color? I am interested in the locations where a woman's individuation path intersects with a desire for freedom.

In this book, I explored the life of Anaïs Nin, a literary mother to me, and her own mother, Rosa Celeste Culmell Vaurigaud. I also comparatively looked at my personal mother, Ramona Martinez, as well as my own life. I am interested in the ways that our creative lives are inextricably intertwined with our mothers. I considered the formative affinity between daughters and mothers and how mothers shape our views and attitudes towards feminism and creativity. Also, I focused on the initiation process of uncovering the psychological patterns of thought and experiences that set women onto the path towards embracing their innermost uniqueness, a necessary aspect of coming into selfhood. What interested me the most has been identifying the moments and experiences that reveal the intricate, and, at times, chaotic process of freeing ourselves and others from oppression, so that we have more agency to shape our lives. It is like pinpointing the pivotal moments of an initiation, a descent into a feminine spirit along the individuation path. As the lives of the women here reveal, individuation is not just about drifting in life while adapting to patriarchal demands. Instead, for a woman to become the unique individual according to her soul, we must be willing to deconstruct and rewrite the harmful narratives and re-vision the detrimental material aspects, such as social and economic instability, that so often have shaped women's lives. It is crucial to remember that the healing and honoring of the feminine within our individual lives is fed into the heart of our communities. Our relational nature means that our lives are only complete in a community. We individuate in relationship to others (Jung, *CW* "Definitions" 291). Therefore, by honoring the feminine in our lives, we support our collective healing. As we become more aware of ourselves through the stories, mishaps and experiences of others, our own individuation becomes possible through a process of self-discovery.

I want to emphasize that contextualizing the pivotal plight of womanhood through the cultural modes of power, including psychological and creative tensions, is not to suggest that women's lives are predetermined and reductive. It is true that, in many instances, being excluded from the patrimony and denied access to our matrilineal legacies has freed up women to create something of their own. Yet, we also know that, historically, women have had very different bases to author their own stories and their own freedom in life. It is important that we continue advocating, soliciting, and bearing witness to stories as to how women create paths that, in essence, re-orientate us around grief and disempowering beliefs that have been passed down to us. By searching and finding our matrilineal legacies, we can restore a connection to feminine ways of knowing and ways of being.

Re-mapping, for me, has become a metaphor. It has provided a framework for me to inquire, locate and spark my curiosity. Re-mapping allows me to study my history, in particular my matrilineal lineage, both literary and personal. Doing so soothes the fears of being lost and quells a longing for discovery of the feminine essence of my own life. Women have long been heeding to this quest, the need to discover, rediscover and honor the yearning to know the sacredness of the feminine, to help better know who we are. We long for the stories (mythos) and *herstories* of the varied contours of women's lives and of their creative expressions. I have learned the importance of tending to my longing for stories, images and myths which name embodiment, creativity and strength as multifariously feminine. That is why I have followed an inner impulse to explore the topic of womanhood and their paths towards finding expressions of their authentic self. This book reflects my own intellectual, psychological, and cultural proximity to the feminine, and my embodied yearning to be in relation with a matrilineal legacy.

The Parameters of a Mother-Map

Re-mapping is an expression of claiming and revealing the contours of both real and imaginative lands. Straight away, to experience landscapes through people, memories, and the imagination, I am held to the same constraints of the Mercator project:[1] aware that every map will contain limits, as it is impossible to reduce a complex three-dimensional sphere into a flat two-dimensional page of a map. Maps are selective as to what they choose to represent. Inevitably, while some areas on a map may appear stretched out, others may be depicted as rippled. Similarly, what I have included in this mother-map, woven through both research and storytelling, is merely the scope of my own awareness at the time of my writing. I write as a Latina, cisgender, straight, educated, middle-class woman. For this reason, I am limited by my own subject position, so my experiences do not speak for everyone. While this map was created from alternative points of views and drawn from a scope of femininity, it is still an approximation. The insights included in this book represent a moment-in-time, a mere stop on an on-going journey, rather than a complete destination. Still, this mother-map provides a vantage to make possibilities visible where, to me, they did not exist before. I offer you insights into my personal story, observations, and the benefits of what I have studied, in hopes that my work will help you through the twists and turns of your own individuation path. The first two chapters in this book contain a stronger slant towards academic discourse, while the second part of this book leans more toward the style of creative non-fiction. I invite you to approach this book in a way that best suits your curiosity and interests. It is my hope that this work will join the polyphony of voices sharing individuation stories, as we continue finding ways to honor the courage and beautiful humanity in our matrilineal legacies. This inner connection is essential for many of us; it is the path that invites us to not only deconstruct our identities as "daughters of the patriarchy,[2]" but also sets us on a path towards healing the wounded feminine in our lives.

While the practice of cartography provided ways for the colonizer to claim territories, this mother-map takes back, renames and resurveys *herstories* of resistance. In this way, I follow in the direction toward which Gloria Anzaldúa bravely set out, as expressed in the epigraph of this preface: "My Chicana identity is grounded in the Indian woman's history of resistance" (*Borderlands* 43). While the urge to pursue the creative impulse is never static or satisfied, I have been able to lift my own disorientation by inscribing new meaning to experiences and landscapes, both literary and real. Through these actions, I have been inspired to "ground" my own identity in "woman's history of resistance."

Holding Hope in Refusal to Despair

Being a woman has long been a political act in society. As I completed the final manuscript for this book, a presidential campaign in the United States was in full swing. The stakes had never been higher in my lifetime; the threat of Donald Trump returning to the presidency was a very real and terrifying possibility. As his campaign based in falsehoods and vitriol gained momentum, the risk of narrowly defining womanhood, including our right to decide whether to have children, persisted. The MAGA (Make American Great Again) movement threatened to turn the clock back on women's rights, gender roles, and environmental policies. He pledged to abolish the Department of Education, upend the Department of Justice, and restrict academic freedom.

On the other hand, we had the real possibility for the first female president and the first female president of color, Kamala Harris. She campaigned on protecting democracy and reproductive freedom, among a crucial and broad governing vision. Harris's campaign offered a fresh vision for a future where presidential values would include a feminine sensitivity, away from toxic masculinity and backward-thinking. While we need inner shifts to create greater consciousness and collective healing, through Harris's leadership we had the strong likelihood of maintaining momentum for the "revolution of the heart" proposed by activist and author Valarie Kaur. This is, "a new way of being and seeing that leaves no one outside our circle of care. A love without limit. Revolutionary love" (xv).

When this book went to press, the United States presidential results were known. We witnessed the possibility of the first female president and the first female president of color be swept away by a candidate who campaigned on misogynist and racist slogans and values, and misinformation. The people had spoken about whom they wanted as a leader. The piercing questions in my mind, among many, are how do we remain optimistic and resist amid all the threats we live under: the rise of authoritarianism, climate change, economic inequalities, reproductive rights, inhumane immigration policies, wars, racism and misogyny? What will resistance look like moving forward? Perhaps some people would have interpreted a Kamala win as a sign of progress, yet one that would have instilled complacency, even providing a form of false hope.

As democracies will continue to be manipulated, it is of paramount importance that we each identify the form of resistance that considers the complexities of our lives against the threats we live under. While we cannot take comfort, nor believe the work of challenging oppressive patriarchal systems is headed towards progress, we must continue to find ways to ground ourselves in optimism and a refusal to despair. Anaïs Nin, in "Refusal to Despair," argued that, in the post war era, it was as important for one to live within history as well as to step outside of it (Nin 6). "We have to step out of it in order to find the strength with which to participate in it, with which to live in it …" Nin writes (Nin 6). She reminds us that what we bring "to the communal life was really the summary of our own self-development, [our] own growth, and that the more we bring something that we have already worked out to the collective life, the more we bring to this mass movement" (Nin 13–14). Living in history brings with it a certain level of anguish, making it ever crucial to nourish and know how and when it is time to dwell in the "recharging power in ourselves" (Nin 15).

I have come to realize that one of the ways to refuse falling into hopelessness during these times is by creating from my interactions with the tensions in my life and issues we are living in history. I rely on the possibility of the transformative impacts of inner discoveries. I can also remain optimistic in my ability to create an unwavering connection to eros, as in deep love, to brace me during difficult times. I strive to relate to others from that place. When we work towards a greater consciousness of our own, we support the growth of those around us. I hear echoes of this sentiment in Nin's rumination that "[w]hatever the individual does for himself and by himself is something that ultimately flows back again like a river into the collective unconscious" (7). Individuation, after all, is interactive. It unfolds within oneself, as we live alongside each other.

It is my hope that the research and stories surrounding womanhood, creativity, and the significance of matrilineal legacies, written about in this book, will offer insights and inspire conversations about how we access and support the feminine creative essence of our being. Being a woman will continue being a political act. Still, I want to stand with the conviction that we will persist in our individual and collective efforts towards building a society composed of a healthy polis that is more conscious, and more capable of evaluating the consequences of their choices of our leaders.

Notes

1 In 1564 Gerardus Mercator created a flattened version of a cylinder map.
2 In her work *Descent to the Goddess* Sylvia Brinton Perera describes "daughters of the patriarchy" as "the woman who has a poor relation to the mother, … who tends to find her fulfillment though the father or male beloved. She may be a woman who can find no relation to the Demeter–Kore myth because she 'cannot believe' … that 'any mother would be there to mourn or to receive' her again if she vanished into a crevasse" (11).

References

Anzaldúa, Gloria. *Borderlands/La Frontera: The New Mestiza*. San Francisco. Aunt Lute Books. 1999.

Jung, C. G. "Definitions." *The Collected Works of C. G. Jung: Vol. 6. Psychological Types*. Ed. Gerhard Adler and R. F. C. Hull. Princeton. Princeton University Press. 1971. (Original work published 1921).

Kaur, Valarie. *See No Stranger: A Memoir and Manifesto of Revolutionary Love*. New York. Random House. 2021.

Nin, Anaïs. "Refusal to Despair." *A Woman Speaks: The Lectures, Seminars, and Interviews of Anaïs Nin*. Ed. Evelyn J. Hinz. Chicago. The Swallow Press. 1975.

Perera, Sylvia Brinton. *Descent to the Goddess: A Way of Initiation for Women*. Toronto. Inner City Books. 1981.

Chapter 1

Introduction

To be Indigenous on this Land: Searching for a Matrilineal Legacy

Uncovering the Personal as Literary: Sor Juana Inés de la Cruz, Virginia Woolf and Gloria Anzaldúa

> I entered the convent although I knew the situation had certain characteristics (I speak of secondary qualities, not formal ones) incompatible with my character, but considering the total antipathy I had toward matrimony; the convent was the least disproportionate and most honorable decision I could make to provide the certainty I desired for my salvation and the first (and in the end the most important) obstacle to overcome was to relinquish all the minor defects in my character, such as wanting to live alone, and not wanting any obligatory occupation that would limit the freedom of my studies, or the noise of a community that would interfere with the tranquil silence of my books.
>
> (Sor Juana Inés de la Cruz 163–164)

The poet and essayist Sor Juana Inés de la Cruz wrote in the seventeenth century from my ancestral land where she confronts and names the material conditions that women are bound to in a Mexican patriarchal world. In her time, a woman's "defects" included "wanting to live alone" in the "silence of her books." Sor Juana's essays read like counter-narratives from the seventeenth century, arguing against the patriarchal viewpoint that women's lives could not, and should not, be their own. In 1667, Sor Juana joined the convent of the Carmelites to pursue "salvation." Before that, she ingratiated herself in the vice royal court. Celebrated Chilean poet Gabriela Mistral describes in her essay "Sur Juana Inés de la Cruz" the salons in which Sor Juana partook: "one more course in that elaborately baroque banquet that was colonial life: Inquisition, devout theater and intense chivalry. Juana had to entertain the old rhetoricians, answer their fastidious missives in verse … (46). The privileges that surrounded Sor Juana were by no means cultural or financial assets of her own. She was born an illegitimate child. When she was eight years old, she was sent by her mother to live with her grandfather in Mexico City, where she had access to his library. Later, following his death, she was sent to reside with her wealthy aunt and uncle, the Matas, also in Mexico City (Paz 86–87). Ultimately, the literary legacy that she left to the

DOI: 10.4324/9781003255857-1

world to educate men and women on the plight of womanhood, would be read across colonial Mexico, and still throughout the world today. For Sor Juana and the women of her time, the desire for the freedom of spirit and solitude to create from a feminine subject position, posed a threat to their lives. Her own decision to join the convent was met with moments of doubt and concern, as seen in "Sonnet 149." As a pupil studying the fate of women, Sor Juana's verses capture the "perils" created by patriarchy's "frenzied rage" that forced women into vulnerable corners of society:

> Were the perils of the ocean fully weighted,
> No man would voyage, or, could he but read
> The hidden dangers, knowingly proceed,
> Or dare to bait the bull to frenzied rage.
> Were prudent rider overly dismayed,
> Should he contemplate the fury of his steed
> Or ponder where its headlong course might lead,
> There'd be no reining hand to be obeyed.
> But were there one so daring, one so bold
> That heedless of the danger he might place,
> Upon Apollo's reins, emboldened hand
> To guide the fleeting chariot bathed in gold,
> The diversity of life he would embrace
> And never choose a state to last his span.
>
> (Paz 113)

Yet, knowing the cultural milieu and "dangers" posed by the patriarchal order, which dominated seventeenth-century Mexican society, Sor Juana still wondered if there was "one so daring, one so bold" to live outside of a cloistered life, where "[t]he diversity of life he would embrace / And never choose a state to last his span" (Paz 113). Still, Sor Juana prophesied that women should not avoid writing, despite the harmful material and social deprivations that rendered them vulnerable. She knew that a room of her own – a place where she can be nourished, even a cell within convent walls – was important to a woman coming into her own, centuries before Virginia Woolf wrote *A Room of One's Own*. That dedication to one's craft is vital to spiritual and creative well-being, paving the way for Joan Didion to pen her famous lines, "we tell ourselves stories in order to live" (11). Anticipating modern feminism, Sor Juana defended women, only to remind us that we must not lose sight of the dilemmas posed by the patriarchy on our imagination as we create the world we need, and want to live in. She knew a woman's life involved a quest not only to locate a physical place of her own, but she also needed to develop the psychic capacity to occupy that space fully.

Virginia Woolf, centuries later and miles away in England, urged women to examine the importance of a "female literary tradition," in a world which exclude them. In "Professions for Women," Woolf defended:

> To discuss and define them [inner phantoms and obstacles] is I think of great value and importance; for thus only can the labour be shared, the difficulties be solved. But besides this, it is necessary also to discuss the ends and the aims for which we are fighting, for which we are doing battle with these formidable obstacles. Those aims cannot be taken for granted; they must be perpetually questioned and examined.
>
> (241)

While women in every generation will want to heed Woolf's call to examine the nature of the female experience through art, not every woman will have the means to do so. Also with the passing years, iterations and descriptions of the female condition will fade away, resulting in a perpetual need with every generation to reexamine the female condition. To put it another way, there is still an urgent need, as Woolf notes, for women to write their own stories about the ways in which we are battling with our respective and collective "formidable obstacles." In this way, as we examine our lives as women, "the labour [is] shared," and we buttress each other's autonomy, helping transform each other's lives.

Woolf's seminal work *A Room of One's Own* provides a context for the importance of a feminine literary lineage for the female writer. Woolf argues that we need female models and mentors so that we may witness the fact that literary masterpieces are not "solitary births" (71). We need to understand the history and beauty of the female imagination. Importantly, we must acknowledge that artistic expressions, and acts, do not happen in isolation, but rather through many years, and perhaps even generations of thinking and tending to creativity. For centuries, women have been fighting to have their history told and their voices heard. Woolf's credo argues that women must have access to women-centered inspiration, including our personal experiences and memories linked to our matrilineal legacies, as stated in her famously quoted line: "A woman writing thinks back through her mothers" (106). Woolf speaks to the fact that for many of us, the need to express ourselves arises from the same yearning to be intimate with a matrilineal lineage. This means that when we restore our proximity to a matrilineal line, we gain deeper access to the female imagination.

A central idea in Woolf's essay "Women in Fiction" focuses on the importance of knowing our mothers' histories. She explains, "Of our fathers we know always some fact, some distinctions. They were soldiers, or they were sailors ... But of our mothers, our grandmothers, our great grandmothers, what remains? Nothing but a tradition. One was beautiful, one was red-haired" (44). Woolf recognizes the need to fill in the gaps in our knowledge of our mothers' histories not only to balance all of what we know of our patrilineal, but to draw upon both tapped and untapped creativity. She writes: "it is only when we know what were the conditions of the average woman's life ... that we can account for the success or failure of the extraordinary woman as a writer" (44). We need a baseline as a reference point from which to compare an "extraordinary woman." Then we can ask: did she succeed in the pursuit of freedom and in uplifting the lives of the "average woman's life"? Woolf knew the importance of expanding the historical record of women's lives, including our mothers. She believed in our capacity to nurture one another. Woolf herself reclaims her mother through her memory in "A Sketch of the Past." She fondly remembers her mother, Julia Duckworth Stephen, in relationship to how she felt when receiving her mother's support of her own writing:

> Never shall I forget my extremity of pleasure – it was like being a violin and being played upon – when I found that she had sent a story of mine to Madge Symonds; it was so imaginative, she said; it was about souls flying round and choosing bodies to be born into.
>
> ("A Sketch of the Past" 95)

In *Mothers of the Mind*, writing about Woolf's relationship with her mother, Rachel Trethewey affirms that "Julia was her daughter's first critic, and Virginia craved her approval" (45).[1] Julia was the one who encouraged Woolf's early interest in literature (44). Also of interest is that although Julia was a nurse, she was also a writer. Trethewey describes Julia's writerly interests as being closer along the lines of "practical rather than artistic" (62). Julia wrote a book on the sensitivities of being a nurse. It was titled *Notes from Sick Rooms* (1883), and it solicited positive responses from readers at the time of its publication (62).

Moreover, despite Woolf's open references and efforts to advocate for the experiences of "the average woman," I cannot help but feel that in a socially divided Victorian society, Woolf would have overlooked women like my mother and my grandmother who grew up in Mexico in poverty. Thus, thinking back through my own matrilineal line, literary and personal, I look for ways to investigate this complex legacy and to protect the right of all women to tell their stories. If we are to deepen our understanding of the multifarious experiences of womanhood and our capacity to face life, we must consider the "average woman's life," including those of our own living ancestors. By connecting to our own cultural histories, familial realities and creative expressions, we can bolster our global community.

The Archetypal Quest for the Matrilineal as a Signpost on the Individuation Path

While I have drawn sustenance from Woolf's ideas, my personal quest to unearth female voices, including my own, is also informed, inspired and complemented by Gloria Anzaldúa's groundbreaking work. In particular, in

Borderlands/La Frontera Anzaldúa advocates that we engage in the process of reclaiming one's own voice by way of bringing consciousness to all aspects of one's identity, even the ones that seem to clash. The way to do this, she argues, is by making "a new culture – *una cultura mestiza*" (44). She writes that this new *cultura* is created, "with my own lumber, my own bricks and mortar and my own feminist architecture" (44). Anzaldúa reminds women of color that we create our own "feminist architecture," by way of accessing ancestral wisdom from those who are indigenous to this land. We must embody the knowledge that is our sacred connection to the earth. Yet, since our link to our matrilineage has been interrupted by way of colonization, we must re-map our respective, and unfolding, individuation paths for ourselves and for each other to claim our matrilineal legacies and feminine truths.

Women of color have endured a double silencing on this land. Therefore, accessing and re-mapping our individuation stories, including the grief of our matrilineal lineage is a form of what Francis Weller calls "ancestral soul retrieval" (51). To not take for granted the questions and experiences of women's individuation, I heed the calls of Sor Juana Inez de la Cruz, Virginia Woolf and Gloria Anzaldúa, among the other female voices in this work. *A Re-mapping of Womanhood and Creativity: A Literary and Depth Psychological Perspective* is not about naming women's experiences for domination, but it is about creating a map of discoveries to honor and re-claim such pathways to better understand the female condition. This is why I let myself be guided by the need to re-map my own matrilineal legacies, for creating a mother-map to help better familiarize myself with the women's voices that have shaped me. In this way, I am tapping into a long line of individuation quests: those of women before me, including who will survive me.

Individuation: A Psychological Theory

I use the psychological concept of individuation, to not be confused with the notion of individualism, as privileged by an individualist society. In that context, an individualist is one merely identified with the ego. In the life of the individualist, the emphasis is not on developing psychological consciousness nor with linking the newly conscious self with one's community. Instead, individuation is the term that depth psychologist C. G. Jung used to describe the psychological process by which a person becomes a unique individual, as differentiated from others. Jung proposed that, "in general, [individuation] is the process by which individual beings are formed and differentiated; in particular, it is the development of the psychological individual as being distinct from the general, collective psychology" (Jung, "Definitions" 288). Importantly, the term individuation refers to the non-divisible aspect of our being, one in which we are individually in intimate contact with our soul. Speaking to the individual aspect of this deepening psychological process, Jung believed that "every life is the realization of a whole, that is, of a self, for which reason this can also be called 'individuation.' All life is bound to individual carriers who [are] charged with an individual destiny and destination ..." (289). Before expounding on the application of individuation, I propose instead to first consider Jung's explanation on the term individuation.

In its Jungian sense, individuation is a lifelong path toward self-attainment as a psychic reality beyond the ego. This means that individuation is not a single act, but an ongoing process that develops throughout one's life. Marie-Louise von Franz, a Jungian analyst, describes individuation in her work *Individuation in Fairy Tales* as "the psychological process of inner growth and centralization by which the individual finds its own self" (1). Jung used the terms "self" to describe "an ultimately unknowable inner center of the total personality and also the totality itself" (1). The goal of individuation, according to Jungians is to "integrate the unconscious, in bringing together 'conscious' and 'unconscious'" (Jung, "Definitions" 283). We must acknowledge that the world demands us to be responsible for our own freedom, and that it is essential that we support others on their unique individuation paths. Since we are inter-relational beings, "the process of individuation must lead to more intense and broader collective relationships and not to isolation" (289). It follows that individuation progresses through our lives as we engage with one another. Jung puts it this way: "One cannot individuate without being with other human beings ... one can only individuate with or against something or somebody" (293). As we engage in the process of psychological growth in our lives, we do so while living with each other. Therefore, any personal growth that we experience in our lives, also impacts our communities. In her work *Jung, Irigaray, Individuation: Philosophy, Analytical Psychology, and the Question of the Feminine*, Frances Gray writes that "individuation aims at completion and wholeness of an individual self or subject once certain conditions, figured out by a subject, are met. Those conditions include assessing and then addressing one's own status as the subject of individuation ..." (2). The process of individuation, for a great many of us, I argue, involves "addressing," through symbolically re-mapping, the harmful existing patterns from societal predispositions that leads to re-claiming a feminine orientation.

Another compelling idea that Jung puts forth is that individuation is the process by which one becomes aware of the numinous unconsciousness as the center of one's life, instead of being guided by the ego and individualist needs. This psychic process is like living a life of a religious feeling, as in living within a religious myth (Rowland, *Jung: A Feminist Revision* 32–33). This was pivotal to Jung, as he "believed that a person should live within a religious myth as a way of comprehending and permitting the expansion of the unconscious as superior and meaningful" (33). One of the ways that Jung believed we could develop intimacy with the "mythical unconscious," was by "living with, and through, both creation myths of being" (Rowland, *The Ecocritical Psyche* 34). Jung believed that Western society had, for too long, glorified one type of knowledge, one myth – that being Sky Father consciousness. He saw a great need in humanity to embody both: Earth Mother consciousness and Sky Father consciousness, which I will elaborate further in this chapter. My interests lie in the ways that an over-identification with Sky Father consciousness, both culturally and psychologically, negatively impacts women's lives. A discussion about the pathways to consciousness invites us to reconcile the tension between the role and influence of two dominant creation myths. In my previous study, *Anaïs Nin: A Myth of Her Own*, I argued that the literary diaries of Anaïs Nin provide a personal myth that is depicted by using the two types of consciousness, of Earth Mother consciousness and of Sky Father consciousness. In this study, I hope to go further and show how the two ways of thinking about human consciousness relate to individuation in the women's lives I reflect on here. Within that framework, it is important to identify the two dominant myths.

In *The Myth of the Goddess: Evolution of an Image*, Ann Baring and Jules Cashford investigate two key myths central to our human experiences. The original myths and rituals of the Earth goddess "underlie the life of all the agricultural communities in the Bronze Age" (148). This gave rise to a type of knowledge referred to as mythos, meaning, truths found in myth. Through gradual transitions from village and town life to city-state and later empires, a need for society to reorganize itself occurred. It is important to note that the imagery of the goddess is not the same as a woman, as in a matriarchy where the woman is in control. Earth Mother was originally non-gendered, as she was the source of all life (148). Rather, Earth Mother personified the human characteristic for relationship and meaning. But as changes occurred towards the middle of the Bronze Age, "the Mother Goddess recedes into the background as Father Gods begins to move to the center of the stage," write Baring and Cashford (152). With this new shift in human consciousness, the myth of the Goddess, along with her imagery, becomes overshadowed by a new creation myth "in which Father God plays a central role" (Baring and Cashford 152). Sky Father would come to be associated with a form of knowledge that is "made by logical procedures as part of making rationality itself" (Rowland, *The Ecocritical Psyche* 32). In contrast to the representation and emphasis of Earth Mother as non-gendered, Sky Father comes to take a male form, whereupon "[t]he emphasis is no longer on creation emerging from a mother goddess, but on a god separating his parents and so initiating the 'process' of creation" (Baring and Cashford 152). This shift had a profound impact on how the patriarchal order was established and developed into human consciousness, as well as how it sought to obliterate Earth Mother consciousness. Such myths are more about the ways of "being" rather than about stories (Rowland, *The Ecocritical Psyche* 32). As a result of Earth Mother consciousness being replaced with Sky Father consciousness, our ways of being associated with Earth Mother now require intentionality and nurturing to bring us back into a semblance of balance. I hope to weave a thread into my ruminations as to how women get cut off from Earth Mother consciousness when being caught up in the maternal wound.

In *The Ecocritical Psyche*, Susan Rowland writes about the role that these two myths play in defining our culture. She reminds us that myths have been crucial in the structuring of our consciousness. Rowland notes:

> Although the Sky Father came to dominate in the form of monotheism, where God made nature outside of himself, Earth Mother is never entirely eradicated in Western heritage ... These creation stories are not distant legends. Rather they are the technology making human consciousness in Western society today.
>
> (*The Ecocritical Psyche* 32)

We live in a world that privileges Sky Father consciousness, which "sponsors objectivity, discrimination, reason, individualism and an ego designed to be 'separate' from the unconscious as other" (32). The "other" that Rowland refers to "may be other people, other types of creatures, the supernatural or even those bits of us that we want to call 'other' such as the abode of dreams" (32). In patriarchal society, we have been conditioned to overvalue Sky Father consciousness (logos) and neglect Earth Mother consciousness (mythos). According to Jung, an individuated person is, therefore, one in possession of a psyche that can engage both types of creation myths, both ways of being (Earth Mother and Sky Father), to come into one's "authentic 'nature'" (33). In this book I argue that what has also been believed to be as "other" are the creative voices and narratives of our matrilineal line and of our personal matrilineal legacies. By deeply connecting to our matrilineage, we are better able to plant ourselves in our birthright to be indigenous on this land, strengthening our Earth Mother consciousness.

What is the individuation myth that we ascribe to today? For many, it is still the hero's journey, or rather, the heroine's journey, as discussed through proto-typical myths and legends.[2] Although these archetypal voyages towards individuation are profound and complex, they are, at the same time, constrictive. While I do not believe a single template for the dynamic and ongoing process of individuation exists, I do offer individuation narratives that capture the psychological processes manifested by pushing beyond thresholds and pivotal moments, often punctuated by fits and starts, of the individuation paths within the lives of both historical and living women.

Although I began my use of the definition of individuation by describing the term from a Jungian perspective, I use Jung's concept of individuation only as an entry point because I recognizes that his assumptions are expounded from a masculine and ethnocentric perspective. I propose instead, that for the women I write about, their formative life experiences are interwoven into their quest for locating and reinterpreting one's personal matrilineal legacy for deeper self-understanding. Thus, for these women, the individuation path involves the process of unearthing the negative self-assumptions about the feminine from within, that no longer serve one's identity. Instead, negative beliefs are replaced with fresh connections to a matrilineal line, filled with inner strength and with a greater capacity for creative solutions to life's complexities. I consider the ways that our respective individuation paths are powerful links in a chain to building a stronger bond to our collective matrilineal legacies, both living and past. It should be noted that because we can only individuate "with or against something or somebody," the individuation work we do will positively impact our communities (Jung, "Definitions" 293). This means that only when we ourselves are poised for healing and for honoring our own feminine wisdom, then we can help strengthen the lives of those we love and cherish.

A Lexicon for Individuation

Expanding Jung's concept, I find individuation in the *psychological processes* that are revealed when *taking actions* in search of a *deeper consciousness*, the *truths* from which to live more authentically. Individuation *moves* are those taken in *search* of an *innate connection* to *Earth Mother consciousness*, including *experiences with nonhuman nature*. Individuation consists of *crossings* of *thresholds* that *align* us with our *highest potential*, gaining one's *authentic voice*. Individuation unfolds in *sacred moments* where we *show up whole-heartedly* for ourselves and for others. Individuation moments are when we *break silences* and *confront fears*. I suggest that individuation is *grounded* in experiences that develop the capacity to reach into one's *inner resources* by way of *intention, surrender, stillness* and *exhalation*. Individuation is *discernment, dismantling* and *disassembling* the established paradigms that *make old patterns visible*. Individuation, I further propose, is experienced in the *self-seeing incremental moments*, be they *epiphanies*, reached through *contemplative prayer* and *meditation*. Individuation is *claiming oneself* with more precision through *creativity*. This means that *gaining access to deeper knowing* unfolds in the *private moments* of the *embodied breakthroughs* that unfold throughout the *process* of *bringing a new creation* into the world. With each creation, *a new synthesis* occurs out of the *raw material* that is *brought to consciousness through art*. Individuation is the psychological process of *finding ways to live* while *honoring both masculine and feminine principles* from within. Individuation is found in the *psychological processes* of making one's maternal wound conscious.

Some crucial questions that I have include: What are the actions in a woman's life that lead to a deeper embrace of all parts of oneself? What are the material conditions necessary in a woman's life to break the silences no longer needed, which were affiliated with oppression in a patriarchal society? What individuation moves are fitting to women in their personal and communal lives? And, ultimately, what are the actions (both conscious and unconscious) that women have taken to tend to the maternal wound in their lives? I consulted with the women in this book in search of insights from the varied experiences of coming of age, as they moved through the highs and lows of life, deepening consciousness. Through the psychological process of reckoning with these questions, women come to chronicle the distorted ways that we have come to know ourselves in a patriarchally-ordered world, including its hold on our imagination. Reclaiming a mother-line, for many of us, can be a regenerative path towards a wellspring of healing and creative insights.

Las Dos Madres/The Two Mothers

While writing this book, I was in dialogue with *muchas madres*, many mothers, both from the living and the ancestral realm, as they entered the literal and imaginary landscape of this work. Yet, while many gathered around the table of my psyche to offer their wisdom and witticisms, it was Anaïs Nin and my mother who both sat at the head of the table, these seats of "great honor," one at each end of the table. Each of them has become a subject in this work. I am interested in the ways that the intra-psychic realities and social roles have become an inextricable part of their lives. I look at the psychological, cultural and spiritual dynamics of each woman's individual responses and behaviors, as well as the impacts upon their development through consciousness making and re-making. These two women have deciphered the signs, which frequently appeared in the quotidian details of their lives, guiding them through to their own individuation paths. As they learned to follow the yearning to become aware of their own psychology, their individuation stories revealed earthly and embodied wisdom, thus also encouraging us to know our own.

My reverence for literature has inspired the unfolding of my own individuation path. And while there have been many authors who have influenced me, it was Nin's works that have inspired and guided me throughout my life. Through her works and life, I discovered the images, symbols, words and ways of being that have taught me the sagacious insights about womanhood and about the courage required to gain one's own voice – one creative act at a time. Through her guidance, I gained confidence and clarity to heed the call from my ancestral lands. She has taught me the importance of engaging in the creative process as an act of self-renewal. Nin's literary credo provides ways to think about our inner lives, even when it is difficult to see beauty and possibilities, so as to grow into our potential as women.

Nin's path to individuate was set into motion by a longing to search for feminine symbols to anchor her literary credo. At the same time, she sought integral expressions of a feminine voice – for her an authentic embodiment of the feminine. She used her art to rewrite patriarchal images and myths as a path towards consciously creating her own feminine orientation and lineage. The outcome led to a creation of her own literary works and a literary mode that she mastered, hence, the literary diary (this is the subject of Chapter 2). Indeed, Nin's relationship with her own mother was a strong force in shaping her sense of self as a writer. In Chapter 2, I look at Nin's personal journey to engage her creative process, illuminating greater consciousness to her own maternal wound, ultimately to free herself. By including previously unpublished archival material, I look at how Nin's maternal heritage shaped her as a writer.

This book approaches women's lives and work through multiple fronts, as there are many factors interwoven into the mapping of individuation. From within the scope of this study, it is my hope to explore as many interlocking facets as possible from these relationships. I examine what the yearning to reconnect with a matrilineal line looks like for the literary figure in this book (Nin). I also consider the archetypal experiences of the search for the feminine in the life of my living ancestor, (my mother), as well as my own. I am also interested in the nuanced ways that maternal bonds spur our understanding of ourselves and of our creativity.

Creativity is the act of bringing something into existence that did not exist before (Rubin 1–2). Creativity is part of life, and it comes in many forms. There are creative energies that unfold in nature according to unique instincts, such as in the design of a pale green chrysalis suspended under a twig for weeks turning translucent as it transforms into a monarch butterfly; to human artistic accomplishments such as "Las Dos Fridas," Teotihuacán, *There There* and Veuve Clicquot, to name a few. Rick Rubin, in *The Creative Act: A Way of Being*, urges us to "[t]hink of the universe as an eternal creative unfolding" (5). This means that we are surrounded by creativity, as it is realized through an energy field, a pattern, a season, a dance, where an idea is thought of, pursued and brought into fruition. We must each be receptive to the ideas that take up residence inside of us, desiring expression through us. Creative acts go into solving dilemmas in our lives. We express ourselves in the ways that we dress, and how we choose the décor of our spaces. I appreciate Rubin's delineation about the "process of creation" in our daily lives. He writes:

> [r]egardless of whether or not we're formally making art, we are all living as artists. We perceive, filter, and collect data, then curate an experience for ourselves and others based on this information set. Whether we do this consciously or unconsciously, by the mere fact of being alive, we are active participants in the ongoing process of creation.
>
> (2)

Creativity is self-expression as we discover a sense of order in our lives. Expressing our innovations can also be a form of resistance. The way that women create their flavor of resistance takes countless shapes and forms. For my mother, creating a sense of self in her world is essential to her ability to feel deeper into her womanhood. For Nin, and in many ways for me too, creativity is the pursuit of self-expression of personal ideas and feminist thoughts, followed by bringing them into the world, hoping they may be impactful. Here I dwell on creations as artistic forms, as well as the ways that women have come to be brilliant creators of their own lives.

I have long wanted to write about my mother's life as a relic of womanhood. My mother, Ramona Martinez, unlike Anaïs Nin, did not commit her art into books. Her material conditions were difficult because she lived under the oppression of misogyny, and she was not allowed the same privileges and opportunities to establish her own voice. Instead, she went on to give birth to five daughters, each one an ultimate creative act. Her sense of freedom and individuation exists within her biography, and in her lived quotidian experiences. She stitched the tatters of her world back together at every possible opportunity and as best as she could. Her life represents, more realistically the obstacles that women of color and women who have lived through poverty faced, whose lives bore the scars of colonization and struggles for survival. My personal mother's story is also symbolic of those who have been underrepresented in the academy and other white male-dominated institutions. For Ramona Martinez, self-investigation has been the path towards greater self understanding and extracting the shame from her life story to create a de-shaming narrative of her own. A closer look at her life (as written about in Chapter 3) reveals a connection to the earth as the creative and spiritual ground to her inner self. It eventually becomes her greatest unspoken strength. The more I contemplated the topic of the various experiences of women's individuation and of their yearning to find a matrilineal legacy from which to ground, I then realized that I needed to include my mother's story alongside with Nin's and with my own. Including my mother's narrative, as a counter-narrative to the life of Anaïs Nin, enabled me to further elevate her complex and rich life into the historical record.

While maternity is a metaphor for the creative process of my literary influences, it also reflects the sense of empowerment that I have gained from my personal mother. I consider female inheritance and legacy as both literary and literal. This book looks at my preoccupation with both the inner and outer desire to escape the patriarchal values that have shaped my life. It then looks at what it means to ground myself and my voice in a sustainable way, where I can walk towards my deeper psychological truths. In Chapter 4, I reflect on the ways that my exploration of my mother-and-daughter relationship were transformed through seeking a greater understanding of the life of the woman who birthed and raised me. In this way, my work is a field study about the lives of real women who have taken on personal myth-making to forge their own individuation paths, on their own terms, to bravely follow personal truths. The individuation path for women, as demonstrated in the stories here, is connected to mending the disruption caused by a patriarchal-ordered world – one that has wedged itself between our feminine ways of being. Through this book, I hope to communicate, connect and share with a greater community of readers about what I have discovered along this re-mapping process.

The Personal as Rooted in the Archetypal

By rooting our personal experiences in the archetypal and by looking at the archetypes that make up the various experiences of womanhood, we can better appreciate the benefits of understanding our matrilineal legacy. It is important to reckon with both our individual and collective sense of self. When we view our experiences through the lens of archetypal psychology, James Hillman proposes that archetypes "tend to be metaphors rather than things" and allow "psychological understanding at a collective level" (xiii). Archetypes, Jung notes, are "'figurative speech' ... the language of the symbol, the original language of the unconscious and of mankind" (Neumann 15). By giving us a symbolic view that helps us query the deeper structures of our imagination, archetypes connect us to collective experiences.

In this book, I define archetypes as a set of recurring images and patterns within the psyche that animate our ways of knowing and of being, as rooted in our subjective social and cultural history. Because archetypes have flexibility, they are dynamic and not static. They have the ability to express themselves differently in our personal lives and in our individual experiences. An image, for instance, can have archetypal meaning, but the way it plays out in the specificities of a person's life is what gives it the strong potential for a deeper subjective understanding. Jung described archetypes as being "present in every psyche as forms which are unconscious but nonetheless active-living dispositions ... A primordial image is determined as to its content only when it has become conscious and is therefore filled out with the material of conscious experience" (*Four Archetypes* 13). The specificity of the archetype (be it an image or an experience) "is attached to innumerable other factors" that relate to the individual's consciousness, and thus unique life experiences (14). Archetypes live in the psyche and give insight into our personal psychological realities.[3]

Moreover, archetypes are experiences that shape and reshape our consciousness through lived experiences within culturally specific environments. I am interested in studying what archetypes can reveal about female experiences. For example, within the shadow of the devoted daughter archetype is the daughter who jeopardizes her own psychological growth at the expense of her loyalty to a parent(s). The devoted daughter archetype reflects a collective experience, including the conscious experience of being a daughter within one's own specific time and culture context. An example that I discuss in Chapter 2 is the way that Anaïs Nin experienced the devoted daughter archetype specific to her conscious experience with her personal mother. Throughout her life, Nin deeply valued the significance of intimately knowing our multifarious experiences, as captured in the archetypal. She celebrated that "living out [our] universal life" was a purposeful way of knowing our personal experiences, fostering the possibilities for greater intimacy with others (*A Woman Speaks* 227). She also believed that although "the self has to merge with collective interests or general humanity ... it has to exist in order to be able to make a choice and to make a contribution" (161). Nin speaks to the notion that while knowing the archetypal qualities of our experiences has value, ultimately, there must be an inner core from which one could experience the archetypal.

The Mother Archetype

Of interest to my work is a consideration of the mother archetype and its impacts upon our psychology as women. The three characteristics of the mother archetype I consider are drawn from C. G. Jung's work in *Four Archetypes*. It is important to note that Jung believed that the "mother-image in a man's psychology is entirely different in character from a woman's" (3). Here, my focus is on mother–daughter relationships. Aspects of the mother are connected to the personal mother, grandmother, stepmother and mother-in-law; than "any woman with whom a relationship exists," like an ancestor (15). Then, there are the figurative mothers that fall under the category of goddess, like the Mother of God, the Virgin, Sophia, Demeter. Other mothers can be found in symbols that arouse feelings of devotion and awe, including "in things representing the goal of our longing for redemption, such as Paradise, the Kingdom of God ..." (15).

The mother archetype is also associated with places and things that represent fertility and fruitfulness ("a cave, a tree, a spring, a deep well, or to various vessels such as the baptismal font, or to vessel-shaped flowers like the rose or the lotus") (15). The mother archetype has three fundamental aspects: goodness, passion and darkness. On the positive side, the mother is associated with wisdom, spiritual exaltation and instinct. "The places of magical transformation and rebirth, together with the underworld and its inhabitants, are presided over by the mother," writes Jung (16). On the negative side, associated with the mother archetype is anything "secret, hidden, dark; the abyss, the world of the dead, anything that devours, seduces, and poisons, that is terrifying and inescapable like fate" (16).

Like all archetypes, the mother is "more or less universal," and "this image changes markedly when it appears in the individual psyche" (16). The way we experience the mother archetype is inevitably connected to our personal mother. Jung believed "the carrier of the archetype is, in the first place, the personal mother. This is because the child lives, at first, in complete participation with her, in a state of unconscious identity. She is the psyche as well as the physical precondition of the child" (36). In *The Great Mother: An Analysis of the Archetype* Erich Neumann writes:

the child sees the mother as the archetype of the Great Mother, that is, the reality of an all-powerful numinous woman, on whom he is dependent in all things and not the objective reality of his personal mother, this particular historical woman which his mother becomes for him later when his ego and consciousness are more developed.

(15)

The projection is because the positive mother archetype is "the most moving and unforgettable memories of our lives, the mysterious root of all growth and change; the love that means homecoming, shelter, and the long silence from which everything begins and in which everything ends" (Jung, *Four Archetypes* 26). Being held this way by a mother is a human longing. The psychological issues that arise from the maze of the mother archetype is what depth psychology calls the mother complex.

The mother complex has various iterations, as seen in mythological motifs. In *Four Archetypes*, Jung notes that "in the daughter, the mother-complex leads either to a hypertrophy of the feminine side or to its atrophy" (21). A "hypertrophy of the maternal Element," means "an intensification of all female instincts," and the negative side is "seen in the women whose only goal is childbirth" (21). In the latter situation there is an "over-developed eros," wherein "the partner is of secondary importance" (21). In this iteration of the mother complex, the woman, according to Jung, "develops in reaction to a mother who is wholly a thrall of nature, purely instinctive and therefore all devouring" (29). Then there is the "nothing-but daughter" complex, meaning the woman who is "so identified with the mother that her own instincts are paralyzed through projection ..." (31). In this instance, she will identify herself in connection to a male partner. She will "project the gift or talent upon a husband who lacks it himself ..." (31). It should be noted that, the "gifts" here are those in relation to logocentric qualities.

Another iteration is the "negative mother-complex." A woman in this complex will "remain hostile to all that is dark, unclear, and ambiguous, and will cultivate and emphasize everything certain and clear and reasonable" (*Four Archetypes* 33). In other words, the daughter in this complex rejects all things feminine within herself that are associated with the personal mother (33). Jung notes that this resistance to the mother "can sometimes result in a spontaneous development of intellect for the purpose of creating a sphere of interest in which the mother has no place" (25) This stems from the daughter's "own needs and not at all for the sake of a man whom she would like to impress or dazzle by a semblance of intellectual comradeship (25). It is interesting to note that in society, the development of one's intellect is considered a masculine trait. Therefore, women in this complex tend to embrace a life surrounded by masculine instincts, away from her own feminine nature. Moreover, it is significant to note that each complex has intricate nuances, so whether the effect is negative or positive will depend upon how conscious we are of the archetypal presence in our lives. Part of the individuation process involves "dissolv[ing]" the projection of the mother archetype away from the personal mother and to be able to embody the Great Mother (Her) archetype within (18).

Important to my consideration of the mother archetype is the process by which we are able to separate our projection from our personal mothers and instead turn towards a deeper and a more profound experience of the Great Mother archetype within. Further reflecting on this, I recognize Jung's interesting notion that an individuation task is not to deny the mother archetype in our lives, but rather "to dissolve the projection, in order to restore their contents to the individual who has involuntarily lost them by projecting them outside himself" (*Four Archetypes* 18). Jung rightly cautions that placing the "enormous burden of meaning, responsibility, duty, heaven and hell, onto the shoulders of one frail and fallible human being" is vastly unfair. When we stop projecting the mother archetype onto the personal mother, then we alleviate her of this unjust projection and can harness the "contents" of the Great Mother within. On the path towards individuation, Jung reminds us, one can "relieve the human mother of this appalling burden, for our sake as well as hers" (26). However, according to Jung, a "mother complex is not got rid of by blindly reducing the mother to human proportions" (27). To put it another way, he cautioned that if one "blindly" rationalizes this process, we risk "believing exclusively in what is rational" (27). Thus, we risk being deceived into a false belief that we know the whole extent of the mother archetype, including the psychological development of the mother complex. He writes: "The more independent 'reason' pretends to be, the more it turns into sheer intellectuality which puts doctrine in the place of reality and shows us man not as he is but how it wants him to be" (27). His concern was that by "fleshing" out our mothers with human traits, we "run the risk of dissolving the experience 'Mother' into atoms, thus destroying something supremely valuable and throwing away the golden key which a good fairy laid in our cradle" (27). In other words, merely understanding our mother complex from an intellectual capacity could possibly cut us off from the "primordial images of life," that of the Great Mother. Instead, Jung urged us to "remain conscious of the world of the archetype because in it [one] is still a part of Nature and is connected with [one's] own roots" (27). The origins that Jung refers to are those associated with the Great Mother archetype.

While Jung believed that understanding our projection of the mother archetype onto our personal mother had the potential to turn into a "mere intellectual" endeavor, I argue that the psychological process involved is both arduous and life-changing work. Therefore, the considerable efforts required on the path towards pulling back our projections from our personal mothers cannot be overlooked. I argue that we have the potential for consciously healing from how we have projected the mother archetype onto our personal mothers. This same process can help us reclaim our mothers' histories as a regenerative source of creativity. This passage is deeply complex. It is a path towards accessing our inner nourishment to heal our relationship to the feminine within our inner lives, our families and our communities. The process of entering the psychological territory of unpacking difficult memories and trauma of the personal mother is a difficult endeavor that requires courage, care, and the making and re-making of consciousness. By going in search of our mother's truths, by locating them in history, we honor the lives they have lived. Engaging this healing process can act as a doorway toward the mystery of the Great Mother that is alive within our own psyche. We can "remain conscious of the world of the archetype," which Jung ardently believed we needed to psychologically seat us in Nature. Staying conscious of the mother archetype means accessing and claiming the feminine wisdom and creativity that exists from within.

To deepen our understanding of the Great Mother archetype, I briefly turn to Erich Neumann's *The Great Mother: An Analysis of the Archetype*. Neumann refers to the primordial image and archetype of the Great Mother, as documented in analytical psychology; thus, the image is not necessarily a concrete image that exists in space and time. Rather, the Great Mother is "an inward image at work in the human psyche" (3). He explains that the "symbolic expression of this psychic phenomenon is to be found in the figures of the Great Goddess as represented in the myths and artistic creations of mankind" (3). As with other archetypes, the Great Mother archetype, Neumann writes, is "manifested in energetic processes within the psyche, processes that take place both in the unconscious and between the unconscious and consciousness" (3). Neumann tells us that, to "provoke flight, [the Great Mother] must be so striking that it cannot possibly fail to make an impression" (5). Once the projection of this archetype is removed from the personal mother, we open ourselves to the possibilities of experiencing Her in all aspects of goodness, passion and darkness. It is interesting to note that the term "great," describes the aspect of the mother archetype that "expresses the symbolic character of superiority that the archetypal figure possesses in comparison with everything human and with created nature in general" (11). In Chapter 2, I look at how the Great Mother in Her all-powerful numinosity was accessible to Anaïs Nin as she reached the end of her life.

Daughterhood: Healing the Maternal Wound

Our personal mothers leave their psychological imprints on our lives. The first experiences of ourselves and of our surrounding world are through the body and psyche of our mothers. Our mother's psychological reality is passed through the sieve onto our own. Mothers vastly impact our development through ways that support and nourish their child. It is our own mother's warmth and love, after all, that grounds us in our feminine potential to embody self-love. Many of us were birthed by women who were never asked what they wanted, whom they loved, nor taught or allowed to voice their truths. Many of our mothers could not shield themselves from the cruelties nor could they command respect and love. They, themselves, were not nourished by a mother, and in many instances, we have witnessed or experienced mothers who were too busy trying to survive the perils of the patriarchal demands upon their own psyches. These mothers taught their daughters, at best, how to psychologically survive, but not really thrive. Our relationship with our mothers has the power to limit our beliefs about ourselves and also to liberate us from false beliefs (Webster 21). The difficulties daughters face with mothers are expressed through our lives in the maternal wound.

The maternal wound is the pain and grief stemming from the absence of early feminine nourishment in our lives. Bethany Webster, in *Discovering the Inner Mother*, writes, "For every human being, the very first wound of the heart was at the site of the mother, the feminine" (22). We first experience the repression of the feminine in a patriarchal-ordered world through our mother–daughter relationships. Webster describes the "Mother Wound" as "a set of internalized limiting beliefs and patterns that originates from the early dynamics of our mothers that cause problems in many areas of adult life, impacting how we see ourselves, one another, and our potential" (6). Also, the maternal wound is connected to the coping strategies, or lack thereof, that our mothers have relied upon to manage their own maternal wounds. These mechanisms, then, are passed down from generation to generation. By becoming conscious of and tending to our maternal wound, we can grieve for the loss of the feminine ways of being, which many of us have been alienated from in our own lives. Also, by tending this wound, we are positioned to achieve clarity about its impacts upon our early development, and how it continues to influence our adult choices (Webster 21). Healing the maternal wound is work that a daughter must endeavor to achieve wholeness, and as a path towards accessing her creative will. The basis of the maternal wound, writes Webster, is the "corrosive principles of patriarchy," wherein women are meant to think of themselves as "less than" (14). In particular, Webster writes:

> historically patriarchal cultures have not only treated motherhood as a mandate for women, they've also made it oppressive, holding mothers to unreasonable standards … wherein women forgo their dreams, bottle up their desires, and suppress their needs in favor of meeting the cultural ideal of what womanhood should be.
>
> (14)

The emotional pain, depression and anxiety that many women face from the pressures of motherhood is unconsciously passed onto daughters through a form of emotional abandonment (14). We know that mothers "can't be emotionally present when stressed" or entrenched in their own shame or feelings of rejection (14). What happens instead is the child learns to read these signs as "maternal abandonment" (14–15). The impact on daughters "serves as a veil, creating a sense of disconnection and separation from ourselves, from each other, and from life itself," writes Webster (21). I argue that the depth of our individual maternal wound can depend on how severely our mothers were treated in relation to their own mothers, and in turn, their mothers before them. In essence, the intensity of our maternal wound correlates to the extent of the trauma experienced by the preceding feminine ancestors in our personal matrilineal line. This is why we gain new intimacy and have greater capacity for healing the wounded feminine in our ancestral lineage through the means of becoming conscious of our maternal wound.

Moreover, I recognize that the dynamics of writing about painful relationships between mothers and daughters can be taboo in many families as well as in our culture, as a whole. However, if we are to heal the wounds inflicted on us by "the corrosive principles of patriarchy," we must break the silences that women are expected to maintain. I agree with Webster in that "the silence about the truth of mother–daughter relationships is part of what keeps the maternal wound in place, keeping it hidden in shadow, festering, and out of view" (6). This means that the approach towards healing the maternal wound should not be about blaming our mothers, but about living a form of feminism which includes the breaking of the silences that have inhibited our lives. It is about the process of breaking the silences put into place traditionally by the patriarchy. The significance of tending to the maternal wound lies within taking full responsibility to make conscious one's own "challenging emotions that accompany those dynamics for the purpose of healing and self-discovery" (22). We must make the decent into the spirit of the feminine self to access deeper consciousness. This healing and empowerment are ultimately for the daughter (8). Also, while tending the maternal wound is about nurturing ourselves, there are possibilities to restore our relationships to our personal mothers. Here, I offer three narratives of what this healing process has entailed. In Chapter 2, I look at the ways that, in her early life, Anaïs Nin's search for a feminine sensitivity related to the creation of literary images and forms so she could flourish. Later in that chapter, I consider the way that healing the maternal wound for Nin was ultimately set into motion when her mother passed away in 1954. In Chapter 3, I look at my mother's spiritual practices with the Goddess Mother, La Virgen de Guadalupe. I place emphasis on how my mother always returned to La Virgen de Guadalupe for guidance and renewal as her feminine source to help her throughout her life. Third, my own experiences, as written about in Chapter 4, reveal the process of moving towards greater consciousness of my maternal wound, which happens to have unfolded, in part, alongside with my personal mother.

I have long been interested in the topic of womanhood and how we seek mothering, and its elements of the basic support and message of love, confidence and safety, from other sources when raised by mothers who themselves have an untended maternal wound. It is true, as I noted earlier, that to rely on one woman to provide us with feminine nourishment is unrealistic, and, of course, unfair. I appreciate Clarissa Pinkola Estés's wisdom that she writes about having shared with her own daughters: "You are born to one mother, but if you are lucky, you will have more than one. And among them all you will find most of what you need" (179). She continues:

> Your relationships with *todas las madres*, the many mothers, will most likely be ongoing ones, for the need for guidance and advisory is never outgrown, nor, from the point of view of women's deep creative life, should it ever be.
>
> (Estés 179)

These words resonate with me as an adult. And while a younger version of me sensed this in my body, it has taken me decades to unlearn the beliefs instilled in me that my mother was deficient, a wrongful betrayal all these years. I have reached the shores of understanding to embody the kind of motherly love from within – that being necessary to heal my own sense of feminine powerlessness.

Throughout my life, the search for the feminine never stopped, including a yearning to be emotionally close to my personal mother. For a long time in my young adult years, I wondered if this craving to be mothered would ever be satisfied. The way this played out in my life meant going off to college in search of a literary family that spoke about claiming one's feminine empowerment and essence. Then, in graduate school, I continued searching for Her vibration within my courses of literature and art. I hunted for images, metaphors and myths to give me a matrilineal line where I could ground all parts of me, and to especially quell my feelings of ambivalence. I now have the courage, self-compassion and skills to go in the direction of my own personal mother. I finally feel well outfitted to seek greater understanding of the wounds and treasures that reside in my own land. In many ways, matriarchs, their struggles, their mysteries and their complexities, have had a hold on my imagination, and writing this work has been a way to re-map my experiences within a feminine lineage in my life.

I have, for some time, believed that by coming to know about our personal mothers' mythos, their stories and beliefs that make up their sense of self, then we are better equipped to embrace the lives they lived. For many of us, our matrilineal line gives us access to empowerment and creativity. Through writing this book, I found many threads of inspiration and ways towards living a life beyond my maternal wound. In its place, I have found strength by engaging in the retrieval of my mother's life story, as I write about in Chapter 4.

The investigation of my maternal wound has been akin to a descent into the depths where feminine wisdom resides, and where I unearth the remnants of the damage inflicted on my matrilineal line. Only in this way can I integrate the treasures hidden from me. This journey encourages fearlessness, intimacy and vulnerability. It is through these means that we can create the psychic strength for a personal world from which we could center ourselves. Anaïs Nin likens this journey to that of a deep-sea diver. She writes: "Just as the deep-sea diver carries a tank of oxygen, we have to carry the kernel of our individual growth with us into the world in order to withstand the pressures, the shattering pressures of outer experiences" (63). Exploring the truths about our matrilineal line requires us to re-map what we uncover along our respective individuation paths. Then, we must share what we find along the way. I have found that our mothers' stories do more than simply tell a single story. They are narratives that carry a generative force that can guide us towards our own embodiment, teaching us that we have the courage and strength to heal the wounded feminine of our matrilineal legacy. In this sense, I have done what many women have done before me – I set out in search of the Great Mother by using words to create my own mother-map, where I can translate and transform the intergenerational trauma of my matrilineal lineage.

Along the way of making my maternal wound conscious, I became aware of my own internalized shame that lived within my body all these years. In *Shame: The Power of Caring*, Gershen Kaufman points out that "expanding awareness of and discovering the original sources of internalized shame, in conjunction with experiencing the emotional pain associated with defectiveness together, make possible the internalization of new affect-beliefs about the self" (12). By healing our maternal wound and by way of knowing the narratives of strength and individuation of our own ancestral mothers, we can embody "new affect-beliefs about ourselves" (12). We can resist being seduced by patriarchy's narratives (manipulated by our fathers) about our mothers' (and about our own) weaknesses. We know that by taking away our mothers' stories and smearing their lives in shame, patriarchy has stolen our own vigor, sustenance and strength to individuate. These essential ingredients are what we need as women to accomplish the great creative tasks we are here to fulfill.

Once we can move towards healing our maternal wound, can it become possible to pull back our negative projections about our personal mothers. Then the promise to align with the Great Mother within becomes promising. As Jung was keen to note, "individuation is accomplishments through life" (Jung, "Definitions" 284). Healing one's maternal wound is an achievement on the individuation path. It is the kind of healing that returns numinous energy back to oneself (Webster 233). Writing about the process of healing the maternal wound, Webster notes, "slowly, over time, it becomes clear on a direct, visceral level that you are divine and connected to all of life. The medicine is in the wound" (233). Throughout this work, I propose that healing our maternal wound makes it possible to break the cycle of intergenerational trauma around the feminine in our matrilineal line, and to ground ourselves in the feminine center of our creative will.

From Ancestral Trauma to Intergenerational Higher Self

The essence of individuation is to be on a path toward becoming a psychologically whole individual. The healing that we each experience within our own individuation paths ultimately nourishes our capacity to be in closer relationships with others. I propose that when we engage in individuation movements, actions and accomplishments, our lives become poised for healing. In *Break the Cycle: A Guide to Healing Intergenerational Trauma*, Mariel Buqué explains that when we align ourselves for healing, we can connect with our ancestral wisdom, which is our inheritance. Writing about the "intergenerational higher self," she notes:

> Your intergenerational higher self is a place of both self-enlightenment and ancestral enlightenment. Your ancestors' cumulative intentions, wishes, and wisdom are layered on top of your own, to contribute to your intergenerational higher self. When you're attending to your intergenerational higher self, you're in a place that is loving, nurturing, ancestrally wise, and intuitive.
>
> (28–29)

We have long known the impacts of generational trauma in our lives. However, creating sacred space for our matrilineal legacies, along our own self-realization paths, is a way to form secured bonds with our intergenerational higher self – for transforming trauma into healing. *A Re-mapping of Womanhood and Creativity* examines the possibilities present when we are invested in accessing and re-mapping our experiences of womanhood and creativity so we can begin to cherish our matrilineal legacies.

Research as Orientation

As with my literary criticism, my inquiry into the feminine experience required a strong vocation for research. When conducting the research that went into this book, I recalled the word in its playful form, *re-search*, meaning "a searching again for what one has already felt as a call ..." (Romanyshyn xi). This work largely has been about following "a call" to re-map what had been neglected, lost, or marginalized in society. Throughout the investigative process, I was reminded that male institutions, including academia, have too often excluded information about our ancestral mothers and their experiences and creations. In her 2010 essay "A Band of Brothers, a Stream of Sisters," Ursula K. Le Guin writes that what has primarily shaped institutions is "male solidarity," which is hierarchical in its "existence and dominance" (102). As throughout history, "women have too often posed a threat, leading to the 'band of brothers' joining together to present an impermeable front" (102). Female solidarity, instead, "might be better called fluidity – a stream or river rather than a structure" (102). In re-searching for this book, I have compiled different sources of knowledge: oral *testimonios*, literary stories, historical references, myths, depth psychological theories and archetypal patterns that specifically speak of women's psychological experiences.

It is my hope that these inclusions and arrangements of stories and myths that I share will capture the spirit of female solidarity, which "come from the wish and need for mutual aid and, often, the search for freedom from oppression" (102–103). Here I join feminine voices and conversations concerning womanhood and creativity that flow like streams and tributaries into the sea of feminine experiences.

About This Book

I began this book with specific questions about the intersections of individuation, creativity and the maternal wound. In the process of writing this book, I found that the best way I could convey my discoveries and insights about how women have come to re-map their own creative lives, is by not limiting myself to academic discourse. Hence, the prose in this book is a mixture of genres. The early part of this book relies more on research than the second half. And while research permeates every chapter in this book, Chapters 1 and 2 have a stronger academic slant. Chapters 3–6 instead rely on personal experiences, told in the style of creative non-fiction. In this way, the structure of my book tracks my own evolution with the topics I explore. Academic publishing I feel too often calls for strict objectivity, which can result in separation from a personal voice. It was important to me that this book weave in various discourses to include both an in-depth scholarly investigation, as well as emotional and embodied truths, including my own.

In Chapter 1 ("To Be Indigenous on this Land: Searching for a Matrilineal Legacy") I begin by orienting the reader on the lay of the land of this book. I provide an outline of the salient concepts and the cultural context for my examination of experiences of womanhood and creativity. While I initially ground my research and analysis on theories drawn from the field of depth psychology, such as C. G. Jung's concept of individuation, I provide a fresh understanding of how such ideas play out in literature and in the lives of the women I write about here. I expound on the definition and context for the Mother archetype and the maternal wound, and the remaining chapters in this book relate these concepts to the lives of three women: Anaïs Nin, Ramona Martinez and my own.

Chapter 2 ("Feminine Identity and a Matrilineal Legacy in the Life and Work of Anaïs Nin") takes a close look at the cultural and literary context that shaped Anaïs Nin's feminine values that contributed to her literary credo. I dwell on Nin's early literary influences and the social and psychological tensions throughout her life that shaped her work. This chapter has a primarily focus on Nin's relationship with her mother, Rosa Culmell Vaurigaud, a professional, classically trained, singer. By using previously unpublished archival research, I reflect on the ways that her daughter-mother relationship contributed to Nin's feminism, autonomy and strength as a writer. Too often, Nin has been defined through her relationship to her father and the men in her life. Instead, this chapter restores a balance by focusing on Nin's formative affinity with her artist mother and other significant women in her life. With this, I trace the evolution of Nin's artistic values and the noteworthy metaphors that were important to her. This chapter concludes with a tender end-of-life testimony by Cheryle Van Scoy, who tended to Nin at the end of her life.

The focus of Chapter 3 ("The Individuation Path of a Mexican Woman: *Fuerte y Desahogada* (Strong and Undrowned)") is the life of Ramona Martinez, my mother, and her spiritual guide, the goddess mother, La Virgen de Guadalupe. Along with tracing the battles waged on her by the patriarchy, my mother's story is about how a woman from her generation (born in 1939) came to find new footing in life through the creation of her own de-shaming narrative. My research into the cultural and religious icon, the Mother Goddess, La Virgen de Guadalupe, provides a context for the constructs of motherhood that impacted my mother's life, and many women of my mother's generation and heritage.

Early in Chapter 4 ("In Search of My Mother's Mythos"), I focus on the ways that I internalized the cultural constructs and politics that I was first exposed to in my household, and how they shaped my experiences of womanhood. I look at how my maternal wound kept me from identifying with my mother's life as creatively empowering to me. I dwell on the literary mothers that have shaped me, as well as the tensions in my education encircling the intersections in my life. I also explore a reading about the myth of Athena, who, we are told, was born of her father's head, because he had swallowed her mother, and what that tells us about women in search of a matrilineal legacy. This chapter aims to illustrate my experiences of reclaiming the emotional landscape that my mother and I shared throughout my life.

In Chapter 5 ("Seasons of My Discontent"), I look at the grief – ancestral and present-day – that I unearthed throughout the early stages of writing this work. I reflect on the emotional impact upon me from re-mapping the crossings and confluences of my matrilineal line, and the psychological influence of their stories. I aim to show the psychological influences of re-mapping my proximity to my personal mother. I emphasize the symbiotic relationship between my body and the writing process.

A Re-mapping of Womanhood and Creativity: A Literary and Depth Psychological Perspective ends with an Epilogue ("Cartography of the Feminine Gaze") that leans on Natalie Léger's *The White Dress* to contextualize how I came to my mother's story. I share what transpired when my mother read the final draft of Chapter 3, which I wrote based on a series of interviews. I argue that writing women's stories is a way to insist on our point of view being told, our gaze restored. I evoke the life of Italian performance artist Pippa Bacca and make a call for the celebration of "women's histor[ies] of resistance" (Anzaldúa, *Borderlands* 43).

Notes

1 Rachel Trethewey's inspiring work in *Mothers of the Mind* looks closely at the ways in which the lives of Virginia Woolf, Agatha Christie and Sylvia Plath were shaped by their maternal heritage. Trethewey emphasizes that each of these women had a writer as mother. This matrilineal context sheds crucial light on the life and work of these women.
2 See Joseph Campbell's essay "The Self as Hero," in *Pathways to Bliss*, wherein he expounds on the stages of the hero's journey. Also, Estelle Frankel's *From Girl to Goddess: The Heroine's Journey through Myth and Legend*. Her work focuses on the ways that the heroine's journey parallels and deviates from the hero's as proposed by Campbell.
3 Of course, a conversation about an archetypal approach warrants a reflection on how C. G. Jung's early application of archetypes resulted in generalizing and reinforcing social constructs, including for example, gender. Jung's tendency was towards essentialist views of gender, which is exemplified in his view of the anima, a male's archetypal feminine, and the animus, the masculine figure in the psyche of a woman. See Susan Rowland's work *Jung: A Feminist Revision* for an in-depth analysis of Jung's ideas on archetypes.

References

Anzaldúa, Gloria. *Borderlands/La Frontera: The New Mestiza*. San Francisco. Aunt Lute Books. 1999.

Anzaldúa, Gloria. "Speaking in Tongues: A Letter to Third World Women Writers." *This Bridge Called My Back*. Albany. Suny Press. 2015.

Baring, Ann and Jules Cashford. *The Myth of the Goddess: Evolution of an Image*. New York. Penguin Books. 1991.

Buqué. Mariel. *Break the Cycle: A Guide to Healing Intergenerational Trauma*. New York. Dutton. 2024.

Campbell, Joseph. *Pathways to Bliss: Mythology and Personal Transformation*. Novato. New World Library. 2004.

Didion, Joan. *The White Album*. New York. Simon and Schuster. 1979.

Estés, Clarissa Pinkola. *Women who Run with the Wolves: Myths and Stories of the Wild Woman Archetype*. New York. Ballantine Books. 1992.

Frankel, Valerie Estelle. *From Girl to Goddess: The Heroine's Journey through Myth and Legend*. Jefferson. McFarland & Company. 2010.

Gray, Frances. *Jung, Irigaray, Individuation: Philosophy, Analytical Psychology, and the Question of the Feminine*. London. Routledge. 2019.

Hillman, James. *Re-visioning Psychology*. New York. Harper & Row. 1975.

Jung, C. G. "Definitions." *Psychological Types*. The Collected Works of C. G. Jung, vol. 6. Ed. Gerhard Adler and R. F. C. Hull. Princeton. Princeton University Press. 1971. (Original work published 1921).

Jung, C. G. *Four Archetypes: Mother, Rebirth, Spirit, Trickster.* The Collected Works of C. G. Jung, vol. 9, part 1. Bollingen Series XX. Princeton. Princeton University Press. 1969.

Kaufman, Gershen. *Shame: The Power of Caring.* Massachusetts. MasSchenkman Books. 1985.

Le Guin, Ursula K. "A Band of Brothers, a Stream of Sisters." *No Time to Spare.* New York. Mariner Books. 2017.

Mistral, Gabriela. *Women.* New York. White Pine Press. 2000.

Neumann, Erich. *The Great Mother: An Analysis of the Archetype.* Princeton. Princeton University Press. 1963.

Nin, Anaïs. *A Woman Speaks: The Lectures, Seminars, and Interviews of Anaïs Nin.* Ed. Evely J. Hinz. Chicago. The Swallow Press. 1975.

Nin, Anaïs. *In Favor of the Sensitive Man and Other Essays.* New York. The Swallow Press. 1976.

Oropeza, Clara. *Anaïs Nin: A Myth of Her Own.* Abingdon. Routledge. 2018.

Paz, Octavio. *Sor Juana.* Cambridge. The Belknap Press of Harvard. 1988.

Romanyshyn, Robert. D. *The Wounded Researcher: Research with Soul in Mind.* Louisiana. Spring Journal Books. 2007.

Rowland, Susan. *Jung: A Feminist Revision.* Oxford. Polity. 2002.

Rowland, Susan. *The Ecocritical Psyche: Literature, Evolutionary Complexity and Jung.* London. Routledge. 2012.

Rubin, Rick. *The Creative Act: A Way of Being.* New York. Penguin. 2023.

Sor Juana Inés de la Cruz. *Selected Works*: Ed. Edith Grossman. New York. W. W. Norton. 2014.

Trethewey, Rachel. *Mothers of the Mind.* Cheltenham. The History Press. 2023.

Von Franz, Marie-Louise. *Individuation in Fairy Tales.* Boulder. Shambhala. 1990.

Weller, Francis. *Entering the Healing Ground: Grief, Ritual and the Soul of the World.* Santa Rosa. Wisdom Bridge Press. 2011.

Webster, Bethany. *Discovering the Inner Mother: A Guide to Healing the Mother Wound and Claiming Your Personal Power.* New York. William Morrow. 2021.

Woolf, Virginia. *A Room of One's Own.* London. Harcourt Brace & Company. 1929.

Woolf, Virginia. "Professions for Women." *The Death of the Moth & Other Essays.* New York. Harvest Book. 1942.

Woolf, Virginia. "A Sketch of the Past." *Moments of Being: A Collection of Autobiographical Writings.* London. Harvest Books. 1985.

Woolf, Virginia. "Women in Fiction." Women and Writing. London. The Women's Press. 1988.

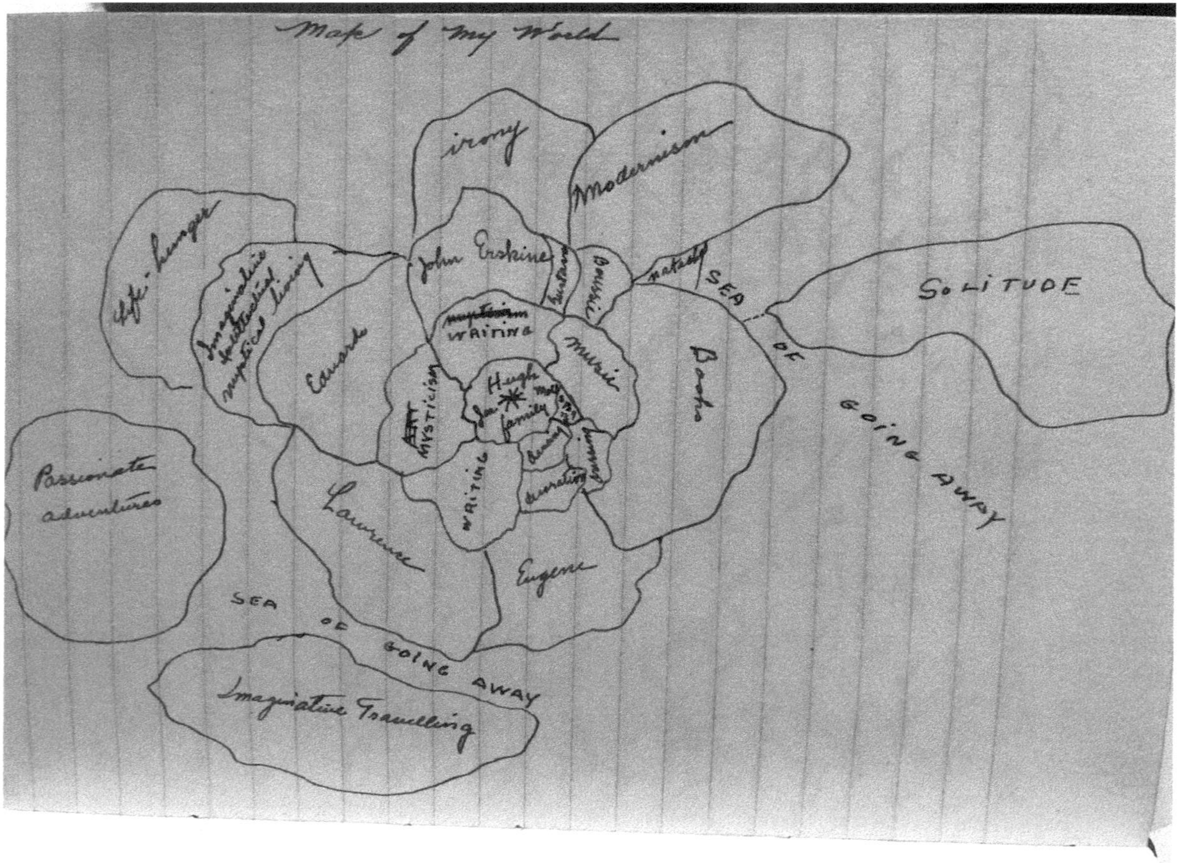

Figure 2.1 "A Map of My World" – a page from Nin's papers depicting the various people and themes in her life, circa 1920s.

Chapter 2

Feminine Identity and a Matrilineal Legacy in the Life and Work of Anaïs Nin

(Cuba, France and the United States)

The first biographical sketch that Anaïs Nin (1903–1977) ever wrote was of her mother, professional Mezzo-soprano singer Rosa Celeste Culmell Vaurigaud (1871–1954). Nin was twelve years old at the time when she wrote a brief depiction of her mother's singing career in hopes that it would be reprinted in leaflets for publicity. Nin described her mother's voice as "harmonious," "sweet," and "smooth," as mere "perfection" (*Linotte* 79). Throughout her career, Rosa had been received with "the warm appreciation that she inspires" (79). A young Nin goes on to describe the social impacts on her mother's singing career:

> Because she is modest, Mrs. Nin remained too long in the shadow of her famous husband. The few times that she sang for friends remain engraved in the memory of those fortunate enough to have heard her … Now that she has come out into the light and been recognized, Mrs. Nin is receiving the praise that she deserves.
>
> (*Linotte* 79)

Nin's earliest writing was to recognize and please her mother. By observing her own mother's life, Nin believed in the talents and greatness of women. Rosa Vaurigaud had appeared before audiences in France, Belgium, Germany, Cuba, Spain and the United States. Yet, while Rosa had the potential to pursue a career as a professional singer, her hopes and dreams were "destroyed by the burden of motherhood and an egocentric husband" (5:199[1]). Her singing, Nin writes, "did not survive. She had to surrender all hope of a career to raise and later support her three children" (5:199). The limitations of the female condition made it so that during Rosa's time women could not simultaneously pursue their art and be a wife and mother. These early experiences with gender roles in relation to her observation of her parents' relationship, lead Nin to define gender in terms of social and cultural roles, which she re-examined throughout her life. While Nin too suffered under the essentialist argument that women can be only one thing (homemaker), she nonetheless dedicated her life to recreating and redefining the female experience, including finding answers to the ways in which women reach

DOI: 10.4324/9781003255857-2

their potential. Nin kept the curiosity and passion of her childhood into the maturity of a woman whose greatest desire was to become a writer.

While much attention has been given to Nin and her relationship to her father, here I focus on Nin's formative affinity with her mother.[2] I analyze how Nin's relationship with her mother contributes to her own understanding of the conditions and autonomy of the female artist. This relationship was not static, and shaped Nin's attitudes towards life, literature and feminism. I examine what a deep dive into Nin's maternal wound, and the path towards healing, reveals about her own journey towards self-realization, including the "thousand revolutions" of a female writer (6:400). Nin's theory of women and writing focused on gaining intimacy with the psychological impacts of the patriarchal social conditions on women. This includes the cultural and family myths we are reared to believe. Nin consistently argued that her role as a writer was to rewrite the cultural myths about womanhood. I suggest throughout this chapter that Nin's redefinition of the female experience reveals the creative and outer workings of the poetics and the individuation of a female artist. Here, I focus on Nin's process of creating a feminine orientation from which to connect her own concepts and ideas, along her individuation path as a writer. I will reflect on what it could mean for Nin to have liberated herself and to what extent she is able to make a lasting connection with a matrilineal legacy, which she set out to create in her literary credo. Through her life's work, Nin, reveals the various ways to map, and re-map, our own place in the world, rather than simply occupying one already prepared for us.

Rosa Celeste Culmell Vaurigaud was born on December 7, 1871 in Cuba.[3] Rosa's mother, Anaïs Pichon Vaurigaud was also born in Cuba, from French ancestry, and married Thorvald Christensen, a Danish immigrant who was appointed Danish royal consul to Cuba in 1891 (1:103). Anaïs and Thorvald had five daughters and two sons. When Rosa was a young adult, her mother left their young family while she went in pursuit of love with another man (5:177). As the eldest daughter, Rosa, who was 15 years old at the time, was expected to step in to help raise her six siblings. She remained unmarried until the age of 30. It was Rosa's conviction to marry for love, as she had "refused to marry rich men, titled men, diplomatic service men, military men" (1:10). One cannot help but wonder if Rosa was rebellious against her mother's fate of having married into wealth and a diplomatic life. Rosa met the one man, an artist, like her, to whom she would dedicate her life, at a music store in Havana. She was there, along with her sister, buying sheet music. The sisters were drawn to the illustrious sound of a piano playing Beethoven's "Moonlight Sonata." Rosa was immediately attracted to the young man behind the piano. "For my mother," Nin writes, "it was love at first sight. For my father I never knew" (1:104). Later, her father tells Nin that "Rosa's sister was prettier, but Rosa had a strength, a courage, a decisiveness I needed" (1:104). Rosa and Joaquín married on April 8, 1902. Later that year, the couple moved to Paris so that Joaquín could study piano and composition at *Schola Cantorum,* where he would later teach. Ten months later, on February 21, 1903, Angela Anaïs Juana Antolina Rosa Edelmira Nin y Culmell was born in

Neuilly, a suburb of Paris. She bears the names of both paternal (Angela) and maternal grandmothers (Anaïs), her mother (Rosa) and her aunts, her mother's sisters. It can be said that Nin carries the strength of her maternal lineage in her name. Rosa was 31 when Nin was born and Joaquín was just 23.

In the telling of her mother and father's love story, there is a tenderness and admiration expressed towards her mother's rebellious actions of following her heart despite societal and familial expectations. Joaquín "did not have the proper clothes." Yet, Rosa decided "he would tutor her in singing. The family opposed their courtship," making her father "desperately unhappy" (1:104). Rosa "faced all opposition courageously, married her penniless musician, and they went off to live in Paris," where the couple mostly lived with a monthly stipend from Rosa's father (1:104). Rosa and Joaquin had two more children together. Joaquin's philandering would continue throughout their 12-year marriage. In 1914 Joaquín went on vacation without his family to Arcachon, France. Soon thereafter, the family joined him by surprise, and subsequently, he left them to return to Brussels, where they lived at the time. Nin's recollection of this encounter was that when the family arrived to meet him, "he made it plain he did not want us" (1:76); he had abandoned the family in Arcachon for good. Nin was nine years old at the time, and this traumatic separation from her father marked her for decades.

Since the early days of her theorizing about literature and herself as a writer, Nin knew that gender was a major equation in shaping the life of the artist. She first experienced this gender disparity while growing up in a household wherein a father's dreams of being a musician were prioritized over a mother's own artistic aspirations as a singer. Witnessing her mother give up her pursuit of her art for marriage and for her children would lead Nin on a life-long quest to interrogate the female condition. In 1932, during a discussion with her then-analyst Dr. René Allendy, Nin tells him she has always feared being "hopelessly dominated by one man" (1:110). She goes on to share with Dr. Allendy that after her parents' divorce, her mother "was never able to love anyone else. She was at his mercy. When he deserted her, her love turned to hatred, but he was still the only man in her life" (1:110). A daughter bearing witness to her mother's "love turned to hatred" is a prevalent theme in Nin's life. When she asked her mother why she had never remarried, her response was: "After living with your father, with your father's charm and his way of making everything wonderful and interesting, his talent for creating illusion, all other men seemed dull and prosaic and shallow" (1:110). Nin's sense of womanhood, as confined within the limiting roles of wife and motherhood, was a deep preoccupation in her own romantic relationships, as well as in her choice to remain child-free.

Early on in her writing life, Nin knew that there was a particular aspect of herself that she needed to understand deeper if she were to pursue her desire to write. This quality and sensitivity that I am referring to was akin to a seed that Nin felt germinating inside of her. For her sense of herself as a female writer depended on its tangible formation. This thematic seed is grounded in gender and, specifically, her notion of a feminine sensitivity within the creation of her personal myth, a personal story told through archetypes and myths.[4] When dealing with her own psychological barriers, inward and outward, Nin discusses the topic of women's intellectual and artistic contributions to society with her then analyst Otto Rank. The exclusion of women from history within a patriarchal world led women (and society at large) to believe that they were too pathological, or too emotional, to have made significant contributions in society. In a diary entry dated November 1933, Nin writes about a conversation with Rank: "Then we talked about the realism of women, and Rank said that perhaps that was why women had never been great artists. They invented nothing. It was a man, not a woman, who invented the soul" (1:291). The "realism" for women at the time was to be a protector of truth as a mother, or a wife, not a creative being in search of knowing and expressing one's imagination. Rank, after all, liked to remind her that "genius is invention" (1:291). It is clear to me that to individuate as an artist, Nin would examine the psychological tensions derived from the assumptions of what it means for women to know their own soul, psychology, and to become intimate with the path towards becoming an artist, more specifically, a female artist who could trust in her own genius to "invent" (1:291). However, Nin questioned what a vow to the creative life would require for women in a patriarchal society.

During the first year of separation from her husband, while he was free from his parental role to pursue his art throughout Europe, Rosa took their three children to live with Joaquín's parents in Barcelona, Spain. Eventually, by earning money by giving singing lessons, Rosa secured an apartment for her young family. Nin records having fond memories of that apartment and how remaining in Barcelona made her feel geographically close to her father:

> From the balcony I could look at the sea and at people walking by, hear the music from the cafés. I began to write poems, memories. I went to a convent and learned Catalan. Letters of instructions came [from her father]. In Barcelona I did not feel my father's absence as final.
>
> (1:202)

At this time, Nin began what would be a long epistolary relationship with her father. The proximity Nin felt to her father, who was still living in Brussels, would soon change when Rosa moved the family across the Atlantic to live in New York. As to what drove this decision, Nin never knew whether it was her mother who made the decision to take the children away from their father, to immerse them in another culture, away from his Latin culture where they would learn a language that he did not know; or whether it was indeed the story that was told throughout the years: that following a visit from her sisters, they convinced Rosa that America was a "better country for a woman alone with three children" (1:202). In New York, Rosa would be closer to her sisters (1:243). Nin's ritual of diary writing began as a recommendation by her mother who gifted her a diary to begin on the voyage to a new country (Nin-Culmell 15). In the early years, Nin used her diary as a letter to keep her father apprised of her life in a new country, as well as a place to record her inner being, where she would cultivate the sensitivity of an artist. She describes the inception of her diary as follows:

> The diary began as a diary of a journey, to record everything for my father. It was written for him, and I had intended to send it to him. It was really a letter, so he could follow us into a strange land, know about us. It was also to be an island, in which I could take refuge in an alien land, write French, think my thoughts, hold on to my soul, to myself.
>
> (1:202)

Nin learned early on that writing was a way to find an inner unity, to find deeper truths to believe in, and essentially to create the world that she wanted to inhabit. On July 26, 1914, at the onset of the First World War, Rosa and her three children made the 13-day voyage aboard the *Montserrat* to live in New York, where they would join her sisters and their respective families. The Culmell family had lived in New York during the Spanish-American War in Cuba when Rosa and her siblings had been educated at the Brentwood Catholic convent in New York. Upon arriving in New York, Rosa performed at Chickering Hall and Town Hall. However, as noted by Joaquin Nin-Culmell,[5] "my mother, immediately when she saw she couldn't educate her three children with her voice, turned to business" (Nin-Culmell 17). For the rest of her life, Rose would prioritize her family's financial needs before pursuing her art.

When she arrived in America, young Anaïs did not speak English. Her primary languages were Spanish and French (1:243). Her mother's educational philosophy was that girls were to be trained in domestic duties. In an interview, Nin described her mother's reaction to Nin's diary writing ritual:

> First of all she said what the Latins always say – that women shouldn't be intellectual. Then she said I was ruining my eyes and I would never find a husband. I should be learning to sew and I should be learning to cook ...
>
> (Hinz, *A Woman Speaks* 170)

However, Nin's writing offered her a refuge to explore the oppressive Latin cultural constructs of her upbringing, defining womanhood in which her life was wedded. She would not be persuaded by her mother about her own future. Rather, Nin believed that "[e]ach one of us must re-create the world" (4:154). She insisted that "art is our only proof of continuity in a life of the spirit ... [o]therwise we would know only humanity's repellent aspects in war and commerce" (5:191). Nin dedicated her life to recording in her diaries, and in her fiction, the life of the female artist seeking her freedom. She created works that depict the female psyche in all its complexities and opulence.

Separation from the Mother

To continue her path of unfolding individuation, Nin would have to confront and struggle against the images of womanhood instilled in her by the cultural values that she observed in her mother's life. Early in her life, Nin became aware of the experiences of womanhood surrounding the all-sacrificing woman. In a diary entry written in 1915, a young Nin writes about when her mother falls ill and she needs to take her place for the day: "I become a cook. I do everything ... It certainly is hard work to take Maman's place and I couldn't have managed it without her counsel. She is teaching me the order that it takes to keep a house" (*Linotte* 51). That same day she draws an image in her diary that captures the tension building between her responsibilities to domestic duties, or to her own art. In the drawing, she is wearing a full-body apron, holding a mop in one hand and a dusting rag in the other, while standing and facing ascending stairs. At the top of the stairs are large, closed double doors. Nin was already contemplating whether writing would be a way out of a life of servitude, as she would state later in her life.

At home, at the age of 12, Nin was taught that women do not sit idle, let alone sit still to dream and create:

> My only pleasure is reading and writing. Maman doesn't like that very much, she says I will never earn any money, but my idea isn't to make money like the Americans ... I just want to be allowed to think and contemplate the landscape and to be left to read in peace, that's the truth.
>
> (*Linotte* 30)

Nin did find the time, and thus opportunities, to feed her voracious appetite to read and write. This was the age when the precocious young Nin set out to write a biography of her mother, as mentioned at the opening of this chapter. In her biography on Nin, Noël Riley Fitch writes: "For years she will vacillate between taking pleasure in feeling useful in her domestic chores ... and fleeing to her books and diary, to her calling as an artist" (25). Nin was often certain that these tensions were her deepest personal failings. Yet, she managed them as captured in this passage. A young Nin reflects, in a passage written in 1918, describing an evening at home with her family. She writes:

> After dinner, everyone settled down in the living room to talk. Then without making any noise, I shut the door so that Maman won't know what I was going to do and I washed the dishes ... then slipped away to write while they were talking "business."
>
> (*Linotte* 352)

Throughout the 1920s and 1930s, Nin uses her writing to help her contend with what it means to have internalized these tensions.

Moreover, an early childhood image and idea that informed Nin's under-standing of creation and womanhood – also posing a threat to being a female artist – was that of the Christian ideal woman: the Virgin Mary. Like my own mother, Nin's life was influenced by the chaste and supreme image of a woman that embodies two irreconcilable ideas: motherhood and virginity. Given the impossible ideal to uphold meant women should renounce their own sexual desires unless for the purpose of procreation, making way for the all-sacrificing wife. While attending Catholic school, Nin was dedicated to the Virgin. She writes about a memorable experience with the Virgin that took place when she "knelt before the statue of the Holy Virgin and prayed":

> [I] asked the Holy Virgin never to let me forget that blessed moment of my First Communion. I prayed for sinners, those at death's door, my country… I asked her to enlighten me in my vocation and in my work. Then I wept again, saying: Oh! Mary, have pity on me.
>
> (*Linotte* 123)

She follows her prayer to the Holy Virgin with a confession, that she has a "great desire to be consumed in love for our savior." She adds, "I wept because I am too small and I would like to suffer greatly, like the martyrs" (*Linotte* 123). A young Nin is enveloped in the beliefs of martyrdom stem-ming from her Catholic upbringing.

Later, as an adult moving towards her individuation as a writer, and writing alongside Henry Miller and Lawrence Durrell, she is haunted by the image of God, a single creator, that she was raised to revere. As an adult, as Nin is working out whom she is becoming, she struggles with no longer believing that there is a single male creator. She reflects: the "act of solitude and pride, this image of God alone making sky, earth, sea, it is this image which has confused woman. (Man too, because he thinks God did it all alone, and he thinks he did it all alone …)" (2:233). Nin, it is clear, needed to believe in her own capacities, as a woman, to be a creator, in her own right.

A central tension in Nin's early life stemmed from the need to find ways to be more than a self-sacrificing wife and mother. She instead wanted to follow her deep desire to assert herself as an artist. Reflecting on the threat that motherhood posed to her freedom, Nin expressed the role that her mother played in this struggle:

> While she was alive, she threatened my aspiration to escape the servitudes of women. Very early I was determined not to be like her but like the women who had enchanted and seduced my father, the mistresses who lured him away from us.
>
> (5:181–182)

Feeling too that her creativity and "aspirations" were threatened by her mother, Nin feared that she would be held back. Also, by observing her mother's position in life, Nin understood the binary choices set out for women in society: one could be either mother or mistress.

Nin's sense of the traditional destiny of a woman to be confined to her home is captured in a passage written in April of 1932:

> My father did not want a girl. My father was over-critical. He was never happy. I never remember a compliment or a caress from him. At home, only scenes, quarrels, beatings. What he meant for my mother I also took for myself.
>
> (1:76)

Nin observed that the abusive treatment that was directed towards her mother was meant, by default of her gender, towards her as well. She ends this reflection by writing: "Yet, I had a hysterical sorrow when he finally abandoned us" (1:76). Nin and her mother were betrayed and abandoned by the man they both loved despite of his abuse and absence. While Rosa herself had grown up in a household of an abandoned parent, she would dedicate her life to her children. A central tension in their mother-daughter relationship was Nin's admiration towards her father, whom she saw as the true artist, living in pursuit of his art. In her mother, she observed the embodiment of the self-sacrificing and nurturing mother. Moreover, Rosa's resentment toward her former husband was palpable, leaving Nin feeling torn between her love for her father, and her loyalty toward her mother.

At age 20, Nin crosses an individuation threshold when, on March 3, 1923, she marries Hugo Guiler, and leaves her mother's home. From Nin's perspective, Rosa experiences Nin's marriage to Hugo (a non-Catholic) as a loss of a daughter. In the spring of 1923, Nin writes, "Mother clings to me. She murmurs vaguely that she has lost her little girl. Of life, which has been all hardness and pain for her, she expected a sole compensation, and she does not have even that" (ED3:2). Despite this being a rite of passage for Nin, one she was expected to embrace, Nin is haunted by the "thought of Mother alone," and writes, "I can have no taste of happiness without intolerable pangs of regret and self-reproach" (2). She wonders if she would have been better off "sacrific[ing] love for her [mother's] sake" (5). Decades later, writing on the loss of her mother's love, Nin reflects: "I asked myself when did my mother's love for me die." She concludes, it was "when I left her house, when I ceased to be her child" (3:114). The threshold of marriage, the opening of a new life for her future with Hugh, was experienced as a loss of love by both mother and daughter:[6] "my mother closed the door on me the day I sought an independent life from her, and after that I spent endless effort and time returning to her, being a good daughter" (5:177). The desire to be a "good daughter" is complicated by her maternal wound. She wants to be "good," especially in moments when she observes her mother appear "innocent" and "delicate" (3:114). These images of her mother complicate her feelings towards her:

As she sat there, trying to work at her bookbinding again, I saw her for the first time in my life, tender, innocent, small. Her body seemed smaller, her hair more delicate. Her great commanding air was gone. Her fierceness gone.

(3:114)

In 1941 Nin records in her diary new feelings of a more realistic image of her mother. Nin sees her mother "wave to [her] from the window as … the mother lioness again who made her children feel like children forever" (3:114). Throughout her life, Nin's attitude in person toward her mother remained soft and endearing, while her written reflections of her are candid, keen and, at times, sharp and critical. Nin spent the next 35 years (1920–1954) trying to earn her mother's approval and ease her own fears of her mother's condescension (5:177).

One way that Nin tries to win her mother's love back is in 1923, shortly after marrying Hugh, she helps arrange her mother's return to Paris, ten years after their arrival in New York. On August 13, 1923, Rosa, accompanied by Joaquín Junior, left New York for Paris; four months later, Nin and Hugh joined them. The decision was a practical one made by the whole family: Rosa would sell her house, pay off creditors, and live with Nin and Hugh's financial support in Paris. Hugh would follow his dream of living in Paris and pursue advancement possibilities at the bank, while Joaquín could study music with conservatory masters at the *Schola Cantorum* in Paris (ED3:54–55, 62).

As for Nin, once in Paris, she would birth a literary credo at the intersections of Modernism, Surrealism and the emerging psychological theories at the time. She would reconnect with her father, who had remained in Europe since he had left his family. Following a 10-year separation, she would be propelled by the courage to confront her paternal wound, and work through the tensions between her romantic ideas of self and becoming oneself, and between societal and cultural conditions of womanhood and her self-creation. A pivotal question she carries with her to France is: will she be "able to steer Mother, to control Father?" (ED3:71). Of course, Nin could be referring to ways to "steer" and "control" the narratives about her relationship to each of her parents, including the wounds they inflicted on her throughout her childhood. These early years in Paris would develop her autonomy as a writer, by developing her psychological understanding of the web of familial wounds preoccupying her at the time. She would have to confront and make conscious her maternal and paternal wounds, including the lasting impact of her father's abandonment on her and her mother. In Paris, Nin will be more resolved to dedicate herself, with her full intellectual vigor, to fight for her freedom to be a writer.[7] While she doesn't have a combative spirit, she has great determination and courage to create the person she wants to be: an artist, creator of her own world. Her close relationship with her mother would continue throughout the Paris years (1924–1938). Nin and Hugh lived in the same apartment building as Rosa and Joaquín on Rue Schoelcher between 1925–1929, and the four of them lived together in Louveciennes on Rue de Montbuisson, from 1930–1935. In the following section, I explore Nin's relationship with her maternal wound and the impacts and creative transformation that tending to it had on her work and identity as a writer.

Tensions between Devotion and Defiance

Nin's devotion to her mother was challenged throughout her life. The tensions between daughter and mother during the years they were in Paris (1924–1938) largely stemmed from feeling that Nin's affinity and loyalty toward each parent could not be met without causing pain to herself as well as to them. Compounding this tension was the residual wound her mother carried from her husband's abandonment of the family. This clashed with Nin's own desire to reconnect with her absent father during these years. In 1924, Nin writes: "What I must do is face the demons of my oversensitive imagination. Half are my own creations and by reasoning I can dispel them. Others, like my feeling of absolute responsibility for Mother's happiness, I must control intelligently" (ED3:64). Nin will act on a resolution, that: "above all things I must not hurt Mother" (ED3:88). During this time, she grapples with her parents' temperaments. She categorizes her father as a narcissist, and Rosa as a steadfast mother (1:220). A twenty-eight-year-old Nin expresses her fear of becoming like her parents. She writes of her anxiety over her likeness to her parents, as she sought to create her own voice outside of her parental world:

> Fear of resembling my parents, whose character I did not admire: in Father I only admired intelligence and feared his cynicism, sophistry, and love of luxury and glory; in Mother I only admired her courage and hard work and kindness but feared her temper, unreasonableness, aggressiveness, and tyranny.
>
> (ED4:440)

For most of her life, Nin sought her mother's approval, admired her "hard work and kindness," yet feared her temper. Learning to disembed the impacts of her mother's temper would be a life-long process.

Nin would further spend the next three decades trying to "control" (and trying to escape) a tendency to sacrifice her happiness for that of her mother's. By early 1927, Nin realizes the role her mother's sacrifices have had on her own life, beyond the mere burden: "And mother had to suffer so that we would possess the heritage of art and intelligence without the evil influence of our father's presence; so that we might know her courage, her power of sacrifice and her devotion ..." (3:266). In this passage, Nin grapples with the tensions between her mother's altruism and self-sacrifice as a measure of motherhood, and her anger toward her father. Nin also sees the courage that mothering takes. By giving her mother credit for what she has done for her family, Nin too can begin to claim courage to move forward on her own path. Nin needs to distinguish between her mother's sacrifice and her bravery to bestow upon her mother the attribute of courage. This way, Nin consciously chooses the same traits to identify within herself.

A greater understanding of the struggle that her absent father had on Nin's early life can be found via a diary entry dated May 1933. Nin writes: "But although he seems submerged in my memory, he is magically ineffaceable. Unconsciously he guides my actions. Consciously I become what my mother wanted, hard-working, helpful, devoted, a housekeeper, a mother, practice bourgeois sobriety, purity, simplicity" (1:220).[8] Nin is coming to terms with a new aspect of her origin story: how her father's abandonment has guided her search for a father "unconsciously," while it is her mother's rearing that has shaped her into how she has come to see herself up until that point. Nin understands that being reared by her mother alone has had the greatest impact, shaping her sense of self, the woman she was becoming. This level of growing consciousness leads Nin to the realization that she had become "a devoted daughter" (1:220).

Yet the conflict of being a devoted daughter to her mother, while still trying to re-establish a relationship with her father, gave rise to great inner turmoil. Nin grappled with the fact that it was her mother who "convinced me that he did not really love me, that now it was a matter of pride to show off his pretty daughter" (1:220). Later, when Joaquín, Sr. was interested in seeing his daughter, Rosa accused him of merely being interested in the satisfaction of the praiseworthy daughter that she alone raised. Still, it is interesting to note that as Nin develops a stronger sense of herself, and gains some autonomy from her mother, her contentment will depend less on her mother's happiness, and more on her own. Nin would take actions towards her own individuation by committing acts of defiance against the values that her mother upheld, essentially the patriarchal values of Catholicism, and the image of women as self-sacrificing. Nin would, instead, dedicate her life to creating the terms of her own relationships with men, including with her art. While Nin would continue to develop her nurturing nature, losing herself in taking care of others, in 1942 she would eventually reach the verge of a nervous breakdown that would lead to a deeper understanding of her relationship to her mother. I will return to these critical points later in this chapter.

A Poetic Quest Towards the Creation of Artistic Values

Nin came of age in a world where intellectual gesturing and creation was relegated to the realm of the masculine. In a diary entry for May 1932, Anaïs Nin, a twenty-nine-year-old burgeoning writer, wonders how to reconcile the conflicting demands in her life to become an artist. Nin sought to know that what she wanted most, to be a writer, was possible. She writes:

> It is not fear that keeps me from gathering myself together and surrendering to one life. It is that there is an Anaïs who cannot bring all the pieces together, who can be devoted, love, and still feel alone and divided.
>
> (1:103)

Nin was keenly aware of the psychological impacts on women in a society that mainly ascribed them the role of motherhood. She also knew that the conflicts she was experiencing were a limiting manifestation of social norms placed on women. While men were allowed, and encouraged, to pursue their dreams, women of her time could not be multiple things at once (wife-artist, artist-mother). With that realization, she deemed it crucial to know how this patriarchal plotting of a woman's life played out in her own psychology. And to get deeper insights into her psychological conflict, she began her first venture into psychoanalysis with Dr. René Allendy, the founder of the French psychoanalytical society. About her first visit with Allendy, Nin wonders:

> Does Dr. Allendy see this, that there is one Anaïs who can be depended on living at Louveciennes a domestic life, filled with duties, devoted to mother, brother, to the past. There is another Anaïs who lives a café life, an artist's life, timeless, not to run away from my father but because I put artistic values above all others. Because writing, for me, is an expanded world, a limitless world, containing all.
>
> (1:103)

This passage reads as Nin's quiet admission to herself that pursuing the path of the artist would require her to not only dedicate herself to developing her craft, but she would also need to create different beliefs than those she was raised to believe. To express her needs and forge a path towards freedom, both personally and within her family life, it was clear to Nin that she would have to prioritize "artistic values above all others." Nin knew that her life's work was akin to setting out on an artistic quest: creating the world in which she wanted to live. Creating artistic values would be a life-long process, akin to the individuation process, with its unique experiences and missteps. If the artist was an uncertain identity, what did that mean for the "artistic values" that she sought to prioritize "above all others"? How would she reconcile all the branches of her life and undo the beliefs that no longer served her, in particular the cultural ones that are insidiously instilled in us by our parents and society? The writer must not only prioritize the need to write, but must have the psychological capacity to follow the inner urge that dwells deep in the psyche.

Nin was keenly aware early on that for the female writer, the vow to undertake the creative life was more complex than for the male writer. The female writer, for example, was subject to the judgements of her male contemporaries on talent at the expense of the restraints on the life of the female writer. In *Women of the Left Bank: Paris, 1900–1940s*, Shari Benstock highlights various ways that women's literary works responded to "the constraints on women's personal growth and provide evidence that documents women's emerging independence and deepened self-awareness" (30). Nin's work substantiates the emotional toll that the creative life took on her, specifically in the 1930s:

> I had one evening of hysteria. A choice between standing in the middle of the room and breaking out into hysterical weeping, or writing. I felt that I would break out in some wild, disruptive fit of blind, furious rebellion against my life, against the domination of man, my desire for a free artist life, my fear of not being physically strong enough for it, my desire to run amuck and my distrust of my judgment of people, of my trusts and faiths, of my impulses. … Then I sat at my typewriter, saying to myself, "write" …
>
> (1:309)

Nin seemed acutely aware that the struggles towards her independence, "against the domination of man" was worth fighting for. Rebellion against social and psychological structures was necessary to free herself and others. Nin's lifelong process would be to negotiate the steps she knew were necessary to undertake a creative life: creative courage, talent, physical stamina and a deep connection to a matrilineal lineage, away from the domination of men (fathers over daughters). This struggle, Nin reminds us, is worth moving through. For it is the effort to free herself from the patriarchal structures, which grounds and empowers her own voice. Therefore, developing "artistic values" means, especially for Nin, becoming attuned to living more purposefully toward fulfilling the quest to be a writer.

The Womb of a Mother and of an Artist

By the early 1930s, Nin perceived motherhood as something that belonged in her life only symbolically. In August 1934, she was expecting a child, which she felt did "not belong" in her life. There were already "too many people to take care of," including Hugo, her mother and brother. She also believed that she already had "too many children" (1:338). The "children" Nin refers to taking care of at the time include the male-centric circle she assisted either financially or emotionally, such as Henry Miller, Gonzalo, Dr. Allendy and

Otto Rank. Nin frames her own beliefs about bringing a child into the world by drawing inspiration from D. H. Lawrence, who once urged: "Do not bring any more children into the world, bring hope" (1:338). In a diary entry of the same month (August 1934), Nin writes a monologue to the fetus explaining the patrilineal world they both belong to and expresses her deep mistrust of fathers:

> You can see by what is happening in the world that there is no father taking care of us. We are all orphans. You will be a child without a father as I was a child without a father. That is why I did all the caring; I nursed the whole world.[9]
>
> (1:339)

Nin suffered life-long impacts of having been abandoned by her father at an early age. This loss was at the root of her preoccupation with the search for the father in her romantic relationships, including the paternal role her psychoanalysts were content to fulfill. For example, shortly after concluding her client-patient relationship with Otto Rank, Nin reflected that she had gone to "Rank to solve my conflict with my father, and only added another father to my life, and another loss" (1:354).

Still talking to the fetus inside of her, Nin focuses on her distrust of her ability to mother a child as she herself still grieves the loss of a father:

> There is still the ghost of a little girl forever wailing inside, wailing the loss of a father ... For as soon as you will be born, just as soon as I was born, man the husband, lover, friend, will leave as my father did.
>
> (1:339)

Nin has deep suspicions of fathers and their inability to stay and raise a child. Instead, a father's life, she believed, was bound to his art. She laments:

> Man is a child, afraid of fatherhood; ... Man is an artist, who needs all the care, all the warmth for himself, as my father did. There is no end to his needs. He needs faith, indulgence, humor; he needs worship, good cooking, ... a mistress, a mother, a sister, a secretary, a friend. He needs to be the only one in the world.
>
> (1:339)

Nin saw husbands as useless with domestic duties and children and who needed to be "worship[ed]." She also knew that the responsibilities of child-rearing overwhelmingly – if not exclusively, fall on women. One of her own fears was mothering those around her, what she considered a weakness. Along with her disbelief in her ability and desire to mother a child, her sense that fathers could not be trusted also informed her decision at the time. She needed instead to believe in her capacity to symbolically mother her own artistic creations. To create her own artistic values required her to assess the masculine-oriented world, including the myths that limit the roots of the female artist.

Nin also theorized, in the early 1930, about the task and destiny of the female writer. In trying to shape a literary tradition to which she could belong, she focuses on gender and claims that the female writer must return to her origins, to her own matrilineal roots where the feminine is a creator. It is important to point out that Nin did not see masculine and feminine principles as fixed into gender identity. In fact, Nin described herself to be "very masculine" when it came to her "literary relationships" (1:215). Nin's literary philosophy was that her work must always be anchored not so much merely to the intellect, but rather, to the body. Nin had just written her book on D. H. Lawrence and, by attributing that feat as the "way out" (of the psychological impacts of the patriarchal constructs for the female writer) we better understand the feeling of liberation she felt both reading and writing about Lawrence's work. In *D. H. Lawrence: An Unprofessional Study*, Nin writes, "to begin to realize Lawrence is to begin immediately to realize philosophy not merely as an intellectual edifice but as a passionate blood-experience" (13). As her literary father, Lawrence's work inspired Nin to imagine her own creative awakening and individuation, and to ground it within her own personal and cultural history. By February 1933, Nin's ardent need to "defend" Lawrence would wane. In a conversation with publisher Bernard Steele when he "mocks" Lawrence, and questions her interests in him, Nin retorts, "Not so much now. He does not need defending any more" (1:177). But in the late 1920s Nin was drawn to his literary style, one that she felt captured "a double current of life: there is the act of living with corresponding articulateness, and there is also the articulateness of dreams, in symbols" (*D. H. Lawrence* 18). She admires Lawrence's conviction to "live deeply" in a world that otherwise insisted on living emotionally disconnected lives (18).

In "A Propos of 'Lady Chatterley's Lover'," Lawrence writes about his observations of a sense of displacement in humanity's relationships with each other and with nature. He writes: "Vitally, the human race is dying. It is like a great uprooted tree, with its roots in the air. We must plant ourselves again in the universe" (Lawrence 330). He emphasizes the detrimental effect of society's isolation from nature and from oneself. Using similar imagery, in a diary entry dated August 1937, Nin claims her own strong stance against the uprootedness stemming from patriarchal values and likens comparable harm to the female writer.

Specifically, she questions the images, symbols and myths available to women: "Man today is like a tree that is withering at the roots. And most women painted and wrote nothing but imitations of phalluses. The world was filled with phalluses, like totem poles, and no womb anywhere" (2:234). In the image of "withering" roots, we can see that Nin is using a similar analogy of nature to echo Lawrence's own critique of the disconnection between mind and body in the dystopia of "man today." Nin furthers her description of the individuation path for writers by including images of a wasteland of trees, whose withered roots have caused them to topple over, looking like mere "totem poles." She sees no bodily connection in the androcentric art that she is exposed to. She is searching for a feminine image of passion and power to anchor her own "artistic values" (1:103). Yet, Nin knew that to orient herself as a writer, to find her own authentic voice, would require her to first locate and then draw upon feminine imagery, constellated from her own psyche, including myths, and the philosophy of the zeitgeist of the era. During the 1930s in Paris, Nin gathered a host of images and a new lexicon to depict a feminine orientation, the basis of her poetic language in her diary and fiction for the unfolding decades.

Re-writing the Myth of the Female Writer

In their own myths, men roam freely. Women, however, cannot blossom in their myths because as Nin writes, "man created a world cut off from nature" (2:234). Thus, women needed to "create within the mystery, storms, terrors, the infernos of sex, the battle against abstractions and art" (2:234). What seems like a natural response, according to Nin, was that a woman instead needs to "sever herself from the myth man creates, from being created by him, she has to struggle with her own cycles, storms, terrors which man does not understand" (2:234). Nin takes her critique and combines it with a deep desire to transform, create and transcend the limitations placed on the psyche of the female artist. If writing was going to be "a way out" of the male-authored myths for women, and its psychological impacts on them, she would need to be anchored to embodied qualities and mythopoetic images.[10] It is unsurprising that the early image that attracts Nin to help her shape her literary credo, is the counterpart of the prototype of the masculine phallus: the womb, "for the womb has dreams" (2:234). The female writer, according to Nin, was linked to an embodied language that holds the fluidity and mystery of the womb, not anchored to preconceived (phallic) structures, or mere intellect (*logos*). The womb, Nin determines, contains the secrets, "a cellular knowing" that is the storehouse of creativity and of the unconscious (*mythos*). In particular, she means women's writing must be rooted in the personal, and the mysteries of the universe, in the "real womb, not in the womb fabricated by man as a substitute" (2:184).

Nin perceives her own art as "different from man's abstractions" (2:233). If a woman is going to create, she must be able to know her dreams and manifest her desires. Nin is formulating a feminist response toward the female artist that offers insights into her evolving attitude towards her mother. The female artist, in Nin's generation, unlike in her mother's, aims at prioritizing her own pursuit of art. She will have to learn how to give her own dreams and body primacy before the needs of others. Gaining her autonomy as a writer was a perpetual struggle for Nin. Throughout her life, she fought to prioritize her creativity, especially the vessel that held her own dreams and creativity, the literary diary. The diary was her womb, the literary form she obsessively tended and mastered throughout her life, the crucible from which her creativity was birthed.[11] By interweaving Nin's family history, we understand that in her literary credo, the personal becomes political.

Nin reminds us that the creative process is akin to embarking on a descent into the psyche, the deep part of the artist, to find the myths, personal images, and languages that can be turned into art, and shared with others. This is the quintessential individual descent that connects to her self created place in the world. Her declaration of the need for the female writer to write from the symbolic womb-space allows Nin to venture into a mythic sensitivity that she needs to ground her voice. It is important to note that this is not the essentialist womb. I argue in my book *Anaïs Nin: A Myth of Her Own* that when we are in contact with the images and symbols found in personal myths, we are often in contact with Earth Mother consciousness. Since "Earth-Mother consciousness precedes the division of gender, we are not merely in the realm of an embodied matriarch, but rather within the 'roots of consciousness in the "womb of the mother" – the human soul'" (Oropeza 31). Diane Richard-Allerdyce interprets Nin's use of the womb as a "metonymy for a linguistically structured unconscious" (182). She writes:

> rather than supportive of an essentialist position, Nin's mothering metaphor and womb imagery points to the creative application of what is itself creative – or structuring, since humans use language to re-create their existence even as they are structured by it.
>
> (182)

Nin believed her writing was an act of intimacy with self and others, an impulse never satisfied. Each creative act, Nin knew, brought forth elements of self-discovery as well as the archetypal aspects of our nature.

Throughout Nin's life, her ideas about women and art, essentially, her literary credo, would continue to evolve. In the spring of 1948, observing the work of the sculptress Cornelia Runyon, Nin reflects:

> It is an act of creativity which remains rooted in nature, more like an act of giving birth. It reminds one of the ancient myth about the image asleep in the block of marble until it is carefully disengaged by the sculptor. The sculptor must himself feel that he is not so much inventing or shaping the curve of a breast or should as delivering the image from its prison.
>
> (5:30–31)

In this passage, Nin ponders a myth that relates creativity with a connection to nature. The artist need not dominate her creative process. Rather, she must pay careful inner-attention and allow herself to be guided by factors not always of her own making: "Everything lies asleep until she touches it like some intuitive mother, and then it discovers its inner life which she has liberated" (5:31). The mother here is not in reference to biology, but rather to a way of being, and of creating.

While there was always a feminine orientation in Nin's writing, her imagery would shift and as captured in the above passage, she emphasized the creative process in relationship to nature, intuition and discovery, a way of being that leads to liberation.

I want to circle back to Woolf's famously quoted line and how I see it resonating with Nin: "A woman writing thinks back through her mothers" (*A Room of One's Own* 106). Nin's iteration of this sentiment seems to be directly linked to the notion that the female writer, along the path of developing her own artistic values, needs to dig deep into a matrilineal heritage, into the archetypal place of an inner mother. While it was under Lawrence's literary influence that Nin awakened to the possibility of creating her own myth from which to write, she was perpetually propelled by her own desire to create a myth for the female writer, guided by her own "artistic values" (1:103). In essence, I do believe that through her writing, as Nin felt herself maturing, through each creative act, she was in communion with the inner mother.

Decades later, in the 1980s Francophone feminist philosophers and important figures like Luce Irigaray and Hélène Cixous questioned the damaging impacts that a monotheistic masculine figure of the creator would have on the feminine psyche.[12] Each of them, in their unique way, argued that women must find a new feminine language and speaking position, breaking the logocentric binary of oppositions (Cixous), and contended that women create a feminine symbology distinct from the masculine (Irigaray). Before these theorists articulated their arguments that women needed to develop an inner feminine authority from their subject positions, Nin, in the 1930s, was exposing and grappling with the challenges a woman's individuation faced inside of a phallocentric world.

Yet, a central tension in Nin's life was maintaining clear boundaries between the needs of other artists, namely the male literati with whom she was in relationship, and her own individuation as an artist. She knew that the resources that are necessary for creativity to flourish, such as the emotional and creative energy, time and financial means, were not endless. In fact, a female artist having to sacrifice her own art for that of her male partner's is the theme of "Hejda," a short story Nin wrote during the 1940s. Indeed, one cannot help but hear echoes of her own mother's life in this story, as well.

Nin's short story "Hejda" was published in a collection of stories entitled *Under a Glass Bell*, first published in 1944. It is a short story about the perils and traps of womanhood. The protagonist, Hejda, a painter, lives in an oppressive patriarchal world that requires women to veil their bodies. While it is her body that must be kept covered, Hejda's voice has also been bound by the oppression:

"Her voice was made small, again as the Chinese make their feet small, small and infantile" (89). As fittingly noted by Diane Richard-Allerdyce in *Anaïs Nin and the Remaking of Self*, Nin links the "physical and social oppression of women to a censoring of their language" (93).

Hejda pursues her interest in art and joins the Academie Julien. There she meets Molnar, a fellow artist. Soon they marry. Immediately, he disapproves of and is critical of her feminine body, namely her breasts. "He is critical of her heaviness. He likes her breasts and will not let her ever show them. They overwhelm him," says the narrator ("Hejda" 90). He "molds her as far as he can into the stylized figures in his paintings," while her canvases appear "childlike standing beside his" (90–91). The critique of Hejda's "childlike" paintings points to her "immaturity" as a creator because unlike Molnar, she has had less opportunities to practice. To her own sensitivity, his paintings are "stage settings, static ships, frozen trees, crystal fairs, the skeleton of pleasure and color" (91). In his paintings she sees nature being "subjugated," and the paintings he creates of her seem abstract and unnatural (90–91). While she turns to her own art as an expression of a sensibility of healing and love, in his work, she sees alienation and abstraction. Hedja embodies Nin's literary credo that art must be anchored to nature. Yet, despite feeling disconnected from his artistic creations, she becomes increasingly absorbed in his paintings. She assumes "the active role in contact with the world" that will help him earn a living from his art (91). Ironically, she has more courage than him to approach the outside world. The narrator informs the reader that "in execution and action she is not timid" (91). In this marriage, however, Hejda becomes the sacrificing artist's wife who gives up her own artistic ambition to promote and nurture her husband's craft. Her hope is that "perhaps Molnar will turn about and protect her. It is the dream of every maternal love: I have filled him with my strength. I have nourished his painting. My painting has passed into his painting" (93). Nin's reference to the "dream of every maternal love" is a critique of the self-sacrificing mother – who was also an artist – by whom she had been reared, and similarly, of the position in which she found herself strapped inside of a patriarchal world. Hejda's life is absorbed by Molnar's success while her own craft is put aside. Giving up too much of herself, Hejda finds herself "broken and weak" (93). She then rationalizes her plight with hope that "perhaps he will be stronger" (93). The story is a critique of the tensions in the life of female artists who must develop their inner confidence to defy the societal expectations to let a man's career supersede hers, or give up her creative will for that of her husband's.

Nonetheless, Nin offers Hejda a necessary pathway back to her art: by separating from Molnar. Only after leaving Molnar does Hejda begin talking about her childhood to heal her own wounds, suggesting that through healing her past, she gains her creative authority. She expands her vision of life; she buys large canvases, consistent with her growing appetite for life and creativity, making herself proud (95). She decides she will "show Molnar that [she] was a better painter!" (95). Now that she is free to create herself authentically, she puts efforts towards female friendships; however, she becomes competitive. This ending suggests that women must seek possibilities for themselves to be free from masculine artistic traditions and forms. The competitive edge is indicative of the few possibilities for female artists to be recognized and valued in a male-dominated world.

"No puedo Más": The Dismantling of Old Beliefs

After nearly two decades of giving herself to the needs of others, Nin feels depleted. In 1942, after seeing several male psychoanalysts, with limited results, Nin began psychoanalysis with her first female analyst, Martha Jaeger, a Jungian (3:226, 239). The impetus for seeing Jaeger was that Nin had reached an emotional breaking point. She describes the moment of "*No puedo más* (I can't bear any more)" as having come forth "with such violence that I broke down" (3:239). Jaeger makes clear for Nin that the psychological and physical pressures that have led up to that moment stemmed from her preoccupation with being the "all-mother, giving out endlessly" (2:240). "You attempted the infinite with a finite human body," Jaeger warns. A significant insight Nin gains through psychoanalysis with Jaeger, another woman whom she respects and trusts she could be vulnerable with, is about her identification with her mother and how it had impacted her life. Leading up to her emotional breaking point, Nin writes:

> I have been more identified with my father than with my mother because he was the artist, and my mother's human qualities (generosity, motherliness, devotion, sacrifice) seemed to me to be a submission to the condition humane rather than a re-creation of it.
>
> (5:132)

It was the artist who Nin believed could "escape slavery through another life" (5:130). This new awareness is a pivotal turning point in her life. As she describes it, "that was the first liberation from the wild, straining heroics. I felt like a convalescent. Weak but peaceful. The nightmare was over" (5:240). And now, at the end of the "nightmare," she steps into the next decade seeking closer proximity toward tending her maternal wound, and to rewriting the myths of her family from this new perspective: "This is a new drama," writes Nin in 1942 (3:240). In this drama, importantly, "the father is absent," as this "one is the drama of the mother of woman" (3:240). Nin reflects on this inflection point in a diary entry dated the Winter of 1942, where she writes:

> It is strange how I turned to the woman and the mother for understanding. I have had all my relationships with men, of all kinds. Now my drama is that of the woman in relation to herself – her conflict between selfishness and individuality, and how to manifest the cosmic consciousness she feels.
>
> (3:241)

Nin explored conflicts with her mother and the symbolical motherhood that she ardently sought to define in relationship to creativity. Through psychoanalysis "as the real thread of Ariadne," specifically with female analysts, first with Dr. Martha Jaeger, and later with Dr. Inge Bogner, Nin reached new shores of understanding what a feminine orientation could be. Through Jaeger's insights, Nin comes to believe that "the cosmic life of a woman run[s] underneath," symbolically meaning the female artist's life is akin to living on a small ship, a barque, near the river. Near the water, she has access to the unconscious. Another metaphor Nin used to describe the extensive capacity of the female psyche was the mermaid. In *The Four-Chambered Heart*, Djuna asserts: "I must be a mermaid, Rango. I have no fear of depths and a great fear of shallow living" (18). Nin explores the power of these metaphorical elements in her next novel-ette, *Seduction of the Minotaur*, which she began writing in the late 1940s. She opens the novelette juxtaposing images of water, a barque and a protagonist trying to give it its proper seabed. The setting of the novelette, the fictional city of Golconda, Mexico, was inspired by Nin's first trip to Mexico in 1947. Nin was marked by the beauty in Mexico, and the sensitivity and sincerity of the Mexican women, men and children whom she met. "I felt a new woman would be born here," writes Nin in her diary while in Mexico (4:225). The woman who will experience a rebirth in Mexico is Lillian, her protagonist. In the following sec-tion, I show how *Seduction of the Minotaur* is a story of Lillian's individuation.[13] Specifically, I am interested in the ways that Lillian explores her maternal wound and learns how to psychologically separate from her mother, rebirthing herself, and gaining autonomy as a woman.

The Maternal Wound in *Seduction of the Minotaur*

Nin exemplifies the newly discovered sensitivity that she describes having gained through psychoanalysis with Jaeger, in *Seduction of the Minotaur*. Self-reflection, engagements with others, and embodiment of a feminine sensitivity are in balance in the novelette. Lillian returns to a womb-like place of pre-consciousness where it is possible to access a pureness with her body. In the tropical environment of Golconda, Lillian encounters within herself, "states of being which resembled the time before the beginning of the world, unformed, undesigned, unseparated. Chaos. Mountains, sea and earth undif-ferentiated, nebulous, intertwined" (83). This place, Golconda, echoes the "first vision" that Nin depicts in *House of Incest*. In the opening of that novelette, Nin evokes a womb-like setting of a "first birth in water," where the narrator sees "things through this curtain of sea" (*House of Incest* 15). Only now, writing *Seduction of the Minotaur* nearly thirty years later, Nin has her protagonist move around in the world where she will "journey homeward" toward the deep feminine understanding of an authentic sense of herself (95).

Seduction of the Minotaur opens by describing Lillian's recurrent dream of herself pushing a ship through city streets. This ship had "determined her course toward the sea, as if she would give this ship, once and for all, its proper sea bed" (5). The boat imagery, themes of life and death, and the need for Lillian to explore both her inner and outer states of being gives the novelette a symmetry and beauty that, upon rereading the novelette over the years, I have always appreciated. This dream image of returning a ship run aground back to the sea also echoes Jung's idiom of the importance of "proceeding from the dream outward," which Nin ardently believed in as well (Hinz, *A Woman Speaks* 135). At the same time, while working on this novelette, Nin had read about an archeological finding of two "ships of Death" that had been unearthed in the Great Pyramid at Giza. It was said that two ships were created to carry the soul of Pharaoh Cheops to the afterlife: "one for the day voyage, and the other for the perilous course through the night realms" (5:193).

Nin described feeling haunted by the images of the two ships and saw a connection between an image in her own dream where she pushed a boat through a "waterless city," (it also reminded her of her obsession with houseboats) (5:193). She was drawn to the idea of two boats being built to carry the two souls, symbolic of two psychological realms, inner and outer reality, one expressed and accessible during the daylight, and the other reachable under the night sky. In fact, the original title Nin had given this novelette was *Solar Barque*. In the novelette, Nin places sharp emphasis on the link between the physical environment and the body, as both are vehicles that move the soul toward greater consciousness. In lyric prose, Nin writes this scene:

> When she washed her clothes in the river she would feel only the flow of the water, the sun on her back. The light of the sun would fill every corner of her mind and create refractions of light and color and send messages to her senses which would dissolve into humid shining fields, purple mountains, and the rhythms of the sea and the Mexican song.
>
> (*Seduction of the Minotaur* 83)

Lillian searches for self-compassion and to restore faith in herself that "had been killed by her parents" (102). One of the pivotal paths towards her individuation is through discerning her self-image, separate from the one that was given to Lillian by her mother. The breakthroughs that happen for Lillian involve finding a greater inner capacity to be amidst feminine energies found in the "chaos" and "dense jungle." From within that feminine space, she reflects on the memories and mystery of one of the most important and informative feminine relationships in her life, the one with her mother: "In this jungle, a pair of eyes, not her own, had followed and found her, her mother's eyes" (84). Lillian comes to a profound realization: she had thus far only seen the world and herself through her mother's perspective, through the maternal "mirror" (81). Lillian recollects her mother, a "tall woman with critical eyes." Using the trope of eyes and mirrors, Nin gives Lillian the necessary conditions of visual self-identification, and thus a path towards accessing her maternal wound.

Lillian recalls her mother's "immaculate dresses" and her style of "tidy hair which the wind could not disarrange," and that her mother never returned her affection "because it threatened this organization" (84). Lillian grows up fearing the definition of womanhood that her mother inculcated in her: "If this is a woman, thought Lillian, I do not want to be one" (84). Throughout her life, her maternal wound had led Lillian to be "impetuous," "excessive," and to have a disposition prone to fits of "exaggerations" and "tumultuous-ness" (84) Yet, while in Mexico, only when "looking into eyes that did not criticize, did she realize she had never yet used her own eyes to look at her-self" (85). This realization leads Lillian on a process of self-inquiry that moves her toward the possibility of recognizing herself as an individual woman, away from the gaze of patriarchal expectations that were instilled in her by the maternal mirror. She questions: "Was this dissatisfaction due to other causes? How could my mother's whistle have penetrated through those underground passages" (81, 89). Lillian comprehends with greater clarity, that the mirror image is an imperfect and inconsistent depiction of herself, and that the gaze can be changed by shedding consciousness onto what it is she sees. Lillian perceives the already recognizable, the psychologically familiar, and understands there is a path toward healing her maternal wound.

As the observer of her own life, Lillian gains a new proximity to herself, and thus to her mother. This new consciousness offers her the possibility of freedom, as she can distance herself from the negative self-images, which she can now claim no longer represent her. This fresh perspective becomes the "interruptive trigger" that makes it possible for Lillian to become aware of herself as an individual, separate from her mother (Gray 76). Realizing the need to see herself in a new light also moves Lillian toward a deeper under-standing of life's "magic formula: life is dreamed, life is a nightmare, you can awaken, and when you awaken you know the monsters were self-created" (88). This "magic formula" echoes Nin's literary credo: through becoming conscious of one's own life, including the haunting past, one may create a livable world.

Lillian's commitment to becoming more conscious of her own inner "monsters" results in an awakening with greater maturity to what narratives, and to whom she will allow to "seduce" her. This is the moment of archetypal significance involved in the process of individuation. This is "the meeting with the minotaur of one's own self, the minotaur whose foreboding countenance we spend so much of our days, and nights, avoiding" (McEville 137). Lillian's newly found capacity to lean into the recollections of her mother, guides her toward a discovery of a feminine way of being. Lillian recognizes the "double exposure created by memory," and chooses to look at her life through "her own eyes" (*Seduction of the Minotaur* 85).

As she moves towards healing her maternal wound, Lillian has an epiphany. She reflects on how it is while growing up, "children changed the size of all they saw, but so did the parents, and they continued to see one *small*" (88). Through this mature understanding, she comes to see her parents as flawed human beings, who can then "assume a natural size" (89). The day following Lillian's epiphany, it is morning, and the narrator states that she has escaped life in the underworld by "return[ing] to life above the ground" (89). Lillian approaches a washstand in the patio and, beyond the picture of cool spring water, is a broken mirror and a community-used towel. Before, she would have hesitated to use the community towel, however, "after the loneliness of the night's journey Lillian was happy to use a collective towel and to see her face in two pieces, which could be made to fit together again" (89). The openness in Lillian's attitude toward the community towel, and the ability to see wholeness in the broken mirror, are symbolic gestures of her growth and newly found inner freedom. In the physically broken mirror, she sees herself as whole, not split off from her matrilineal lineage. Early in the story, while in Mexico, Lillian maintains independence from the novelette's male characters and shares in community events at her own will. However, as Lillian reaches the end of her stay in Golconda, she gains a stronger ability to be in community without the fear of being engulfed by her wounds, or by the wounds of others. With these new insights, Lillian begins to voyage back home, both to herself as well as physically home to her family. At this point in the novelette, Nin's depiction of Lillian is of a mature woman who is now able to reunite with her husband, Larry. In *Collage of Dreams*, Sharon Spencer writes that upon their reunion, Lillian can offer Larry a new love, a love as an equal partner, not the mother's sacrificial love (Spencer 75–76). In this way, Lillian is ready to offer Larry the kind of love that stems from a place of healing and self-compassion.

Further in the novelette, Lillian's quest towards individuation leads her to reflect on how, years prior, she had experienced her mother's death, as a time when "the spirit of her mother had passed into her" (*Seduction of the Minotaur* 101). Lillian ruminates on how she had felt "possessed" by her mother in the ways that she took on some of her "mannerisms and traits (the very ones she had rebelled against while her mother was alive, the very ones which had injured her own growth)" (101). An emotionally blocked Lillian becomes her mother in that she had repeated her mother's psychologically abusive ways onto her own children. Yet, Lillian's new maturity, found in Golconda, allows her to embrace her mother's memory with greater awareness. Through perceptive wisdom, Lillian navigates the labyrinth of her own psyche. In particular, early in the novelette, it is Dr. Hernandez's wisdom, the town doctor, that encourages her to confront the past as a path towards healing. He tells her that the "design" of our psychic wounds, and the role they take in life, is created "from within us. It is internal" (103). Throughout her stay in Golconda, Lillian learns that faith in herself and her relationships is possible through an emotional and spiritual understanding of her maternal wound.

The emotional atmosphere around Lillian's epiphany, as she moves towards healing her maternal wound and gaining autonomy from her mother, bear significant biographical details. Rosa, Nin's mother, died in August 1954 when Nin was 51 years old. (Interestingly, the same age I was when I began interviewing my mother to write Chapter 3 of this book.) Nin's reaction to the pain over losing her mother was, she writes, "deeper than at [her] father's death," for she felt she had not "loved her well enough" (5:181). As Nin grieves the death of her mother, she must also confront the yearning for a strong and lasting connection between mother and daughter, one wherein they would have found mutual support and love for one another, and, in essence, a connection to her maternal legacy. She describes the pain as an "irrevocable loss…a greater and deeper pain because there was no sense of unity, of fusion, of closeness and I had hoped to achieve this" (5:176). She laments that coming "close to her" was a "lifelong struggle" (5:176). Through grieving Rosa's death, Nin contends with not only the loss of a mother, but of the "hope of fulfillment, of union with her, of an understanding, penetrating love" (5:176). In her diary, Nin accesses the emotional truth of the moment: "The loss is greater and more terrible when closeness is not attained. All my life I had struggled to come close to her, and now she was lost to me" (5:177). Throughout her life, Nin's stark, at times paralyzing, fear of her mother's rejection and strong temper left her feeling overwhelmingly vulnerable to her own internalized insecurities and fear of exposing her feminine truths in her writing. Now, while grieving her mother, she comes to a deeper understanding of how her own maternal wound informed the ways that she had "rebelled" against the "ideal figure" in a daughter that a mother desires. In a reflection drawn from the archives, dated Thursday, August 12, 1954, we gain a deeper, emotionally tender and honest understanding of the aspects of her matrilineal lineage from which she had felt she needed to separate. It was Rosa's definition of womanhood that Nin struggled with throughout her life. Nin writes:

> I forfeited this closeness by my rebellion and growth. There was a time before 16, 20 years, even until 26 when I was more like Joaquin … I was close to my mother then, and then I lost her, first by my rebellion against Catholicism at the age of 16, then by my marriage to Hugo and departure from her home, then by my not having children but lovers (who were children). So that I did not treat my lovers in the irresponsible way my father did but as my mother would have treated them.
>
> (Anaïs Nin Papers[14])

In this passage, Nin seems bitter towards the fact that she had felt she needed to "forfeit" being close to her mother in pursuit of her individuation. She reflects on the pivotal moments in her life wherein she defied her mother for the sake of her own developmental growth. Two of those moments are in connection with breaking from oppressive patriarchal values: one, Catholicism, and two, marrying a man of her choice, which was Hugo, a non-Catholic. Also, in this passage, Nin not only admits to having had "lovers," but her true feelings, that they "were children." She seems to be coming to terms with the extent to which she over-extended herself in carrying for them, like a mother does for a child. While there is a similar passage in Nin's expurgated diary Volume 5, it is only a paraphrase of the above. In Volume 5, Nin writes:

> Except from the age of eleven until twenty, when I was completely and utterly devoted to her, thinking only of helping her. But later when I began to grow in a different direction, when I left her house, became independent, then conceding my love and admiration of her would have meant an acceptance of beliefs and attitudes which I considered a threat to my existence.
>
> (5:181)

Both passages were written in August 1954, the year of Rosa's death. The emotional truth that Nin accessed following her mother's death, set into motion the healing of her maternal wound. This newly touched psychological realization is written into Lillian's character, which I return to shortly.

I want to dwell on Nin's reference to a mother's "penetrating love." Nin keenly recognized the impacts of a mother's support on the female artist, sentiments also echoed in Rachel Cusk's article dated May 8, 2023 in the *New York Times Magazine*, "Annie Ernaux Has Broken Every Taboo of What Women are Allowed to Write." Cusk writes about having learned about Ernaux's relationship with her mother. Their mother-daughter relationship was at once strained because of a depiction that Ernaux had written and published about her mother in her early fiction. Yet, despite this friction, a strong bond between mother and daughter prevailed throughout Ernaux's life. In fact, Ernaux tells Cusk that she had her mother's steadfast support and love, a pillar to her own sense of self as a writer. After spending a day with Ernaux in her home in Cergy, France, Cusk comes away pondering the "palpable and forceful aura that emanates from Ernaux... an aura of unbreakable and radiant autonomy" (46). Cusk conjectures that the source of the strength and independence in Ernaux's feminine subjectivity, could likely stem from the "unbreakable gift of love, the motherlove that extends even to forgiving the betrayal that is writing" (46). This "unbreakable" endowment of mother-love that Cusk is referencing seems to relate to a particular feminine strength that buttresses the freedom of the female artist that Nin too sought throughout her life. Cusk's remarks remind me that, for some of us, our mother's support, and often through tending our maternal wound, we women who are coming into our womanhood as writers, can be entrusted with an armoring "against the whole world" (Cusk 46). Cusk suggests certain female artists are indeed reinforced by a strong matrilineal legacy from which she can link her own creative will.

Detachment from a matrilineal line can create instability. Cusk, like Nin, seems to recognize, that the unavailability or absence of a mother's "unbreakable gift of love," especially when withheld due to detrimental impacts of patriarchal constructs of womanhood, can be an inner threat to one's ability to bear witness to our personal truths and vulnerabilities. Without maternal support, the female writer could be left to feel split off from her creative energies. This parallels the ethos in Cusk's points about a common source of women's insecurities. She notes that this could be a "reason each of us have struggled to contain the splintering of our creative energies around personal truth, this elemental fear of disapproval, rejection, abandonment – the grandmother's suggestion that what we're doing isn't very nice" (46). She acknowledges the possibilities for freedom for the female writer when she allows her yearning for expression to be linked to deeply rooted matrilineal legacies of strength and passion. Through this connection, we can better travel towards confronting the internal fear of laying bare onto the page our feminine self, as in who we are, and who we are becoming. Claiming a personal mother's strength and support seems to be a vital foundation of our ability to embody a "radiant autonomy." What prevents the female writer from this possibility, Cusk laments, is that for too long, the female writer has been instead bound to misogyny. Cusk aptly writes: "If it remains difficult for women to make art about their own lives, it is because femininity still has no stable place in culture" (46). The female writer, it is clear, has had to work harder than her male counterpart to find her secure place in the world. A deep yearning to find a stable feminine voice, for many of us, has meant bearing a greater weight of vulnerability.

A Mother's Love, Womanhood and Creativity

Nin felt her creative life was attached to her mother, like each strand of a web. Specifically, Nin feared her mother's harsh judgements, and emotional abandonment throughout her life. Her mother's open disapproval curtailed her artistic self, over and over throughout her life: "My mother wanted me to be someone other than the woman I was. She was shocked when I defended D. H. Lawrence. She disliked my artist friends. She wanted me to be as she had been, essentially maternal" (5:182). Nin writes feeling that "while she was alive, she threatened my aspiration to escape the servitudes of women," and felt her mother "condemned" her freedom (5:182). What was left after her mother's death, Nin explained, was to grieve all her hopes and desires for her mother's "penetrating love" and acceptance. Nin writes:

> When she died I was forced to take into myself this conflict, and I realized I had long ago lost the battle. I am a woman who takes care of others on the same level my mother did. As soon as she died, this rebellion collapsed.
>
> (5:199)

By transcending the rebellious daughter, Nin, like Lilllian, in *Seduction of the Minotaur*, experiences a rebirth: "Surely, our parents give birth to us twice, the second time when they die...we accept the legacy of their character traits" (5:184). Nin's creativity flows, through the acceptance of her own mother's death, and her willingness to embrace her own inner mother. We see in her depiction of Lillian a woman who psychologically evolves as she too grieves the loss of her mother. By working through her negative mother complex, Lillian develops trust in her feminine intuition about her own healing and position in life, both in relationship to her mother, and apart from her mother.

Following her mother's death, Nin reflects on the possible causes of her mother's negative actions towards her children. She contemplates what her mother's life would have been as a child-free woman. She wonders in her diary, "[w]hat would her life have been without children, concertizing, traveling, as pampered by the public as my father was" (5:178). As she grieves her mother, and writes about the emotional reality of her grief, Nin experiences a reawakening of self-love, away from her mother's critical gaze. This psychological insight makes it safe to be who she desired to be as an artist, while also acknowledging the freedom from the weight of her negative emotions surrounding her mother. Nin reflects:

> it was not the loss of my mother which reawakened my love for her, it was because my mother's disappearance removed the stigma of her judgments, the dangers and guilt brought about her by her influence, and left me a simple human being no longer concerned with my own survival, but able to recognize her qualities
>
> (5:182).

No longer "concerned with [her] own survival," Nin can better accept what she inherited from her mother: "a strong protective instinct toward human beings" (5:182). Nin begins the process of coming to terms with the ways in which she has protected "the weak and the helpless" throughout her own life (5:182). She accepts her mother's "legacy," that is, the impacts of her mother's life on her. In essence, Nin taps into her matrilineal legacy of "maternal passion" and a tremendous ability to "care for others." By recognizing the immensity of her mother's courage and generosity, she embraces that her own artistic drive stems from that of her mother's (5:177). Having processed her feelings about her mother's legacy, Nin can better understand her mother's paradoxical qualities, as she writes about in a passage unpublished, but which I located in her archives:

> Her brothers and sisters speak of her as her children do: an impossible temper (*un caracte imposible*) and a heart of gold. Perhaps then, marrying my father (another motherhood) and "sacrificing" her life to her 3 children was what gave her so much anger. She loved to sing. She was sociable, natural, very cheerful when not combative.
>
> (Anaïs Nin Papers)

Vestiges of Nin's concerns over her mother's "*caracte imposible*," "impossible character," permeated her maternal wound. Nin was long aware of the negative impacts that sacrificing her career had on her mother. Nin reminds us that the better we understand the forces that our mothers have navigated, the better we can fully see them. By gaining a greater portrait of her mother's life, Nin grappled with the traits of her matrilineal line. However, rather than continuing to rebel against these traits, she embraced them. It is interesting to note that in Nin's expurgated diaries, we see a similar passage, but with a less critical, tone:

> Her brothers and sisters speak of her as children do: "A tyrant with a heart of gold." Perhaps, then, marrying my father when he was only twenty-two years old and she thirty, another motherhood, and sacrificing her life to her three children may have been what gave her so much anger.
> (5:177)

This passage seems to be extracted from the previously referenced passage I located in the archives. The expurgated passage emphasizes the age difference between her parents, and leaves out "very cheerful when not combative," capturing a more sympathetic tone towards her mother's fate of having to give up her artistry. Reading these two passages side-by-side allow insights into the complexity of Nin's feelings towards her mother, and to the parts of Nin that perhaps always wanted to protect her public portrayal of her relationship with her mother.

Moreover, Nin allows us to see, through her characterization of Lillian, in the novelette, her personal struggles against an internalized negative mother image that she must confront to seek her own individuation. While grieving her mother, and through a new level of self-understanding, Nin questions the extent to which we spend our lives feeling separate from others, enveloped in fear of the cost of intimacy, as she questioned in her diary while writing *Seduction of the Minotaur*: "Why do people carry away with them so great a part of our knowledge of them, of their thoughts and feelings which would make us love them better" (5:177). This is the same probing that Nin's protagonist, Lillian, ponders: "if only human beings did not draw the blinds, don disguises, and live in isolation cells marked: not yet time for revelation …" (*Seduction of the Minotaur* 95). And we know that she has Lillian in mind because in her diary she writes, "I am at work on Lillian's return to her home and children, and in musical terms, Lillian is struggling with the *muted* tones she had not been able to hear" (5:184).

The "*muted* tones," a musical reference, refers to the ways that we struggle to interpret and interact with the wounds and moods of those we love. Too often, Nin reminds us, we are incapable of breaking through the stone walls erected out of our respective wounds, leaving us muted, unable to access the vulnerabilities necessary to create authentic connections.

By giving up the battle of rejecting her mother, Nin and Lillian can both nurture and accept new parts of themselves. In this discovery lies the ability to extend empathy to herself and others. In "Nin, Borgas and Paz: Labyrinthine

Passageways of Mind and Language," Suzanne Nalbantian writes about the importance of Nin's use of memories to evoke healing, seen in both her fiction and diary: "In exposing her deeper memories, her fiction liberates her from the constrictions of the labyrinth which her life and its transcription in the diary had created" (124). In her diaries, Nin expresses long-felt emotions about her maternal wound; in *Seduction of the Minotaur,* she depicts them with greater emotional clarity, laying them to rest.

Years later, reflecting with fresh emotional lucidity towards a sewing machine and gold thimble she had inherited from her mother, Nin writes:

> The spirit of my mother imbedded in her sewing machine and in her gold thimble did not make me love housework. It may have been that my mother's irritation was a clue to her rebellion against the supremacy of the mother role in her, and that what I identified with was a deeper truth I had never seen consciously: A mother who did not want to be a mother all the time, who had to mother a husband, and three young children, who at one time had wanted to be a concert singer.
>
> (6:41)

Her developed insight into the potential rebellion her mother could have felt toward her own experiences with motherhood invites Nin to have a more sympathetic and human depiction of her mother. This is indicative of a newly found capacity to humanize her mother along the path towards healing her maternal wound, a trait of individuation.

Importantly, Nin was aware of the challenges and complexities involved in individuating within our families. In a moving passage dated Fall 1954, she writes: "The loveliest, the most carefree aspects of those we love we are rarely given, because of the conflict we engage in, each one, in each family, to assert our individual existence against the clan's rules and taboos" (5:199). Following her mother's death, Nin continues to gain greater clarity of her own fears and family trauma. In the unfolding years, she travels deeper into the process of rewriting the myth of her family. Nin embraces a yearning to develop her own values away from those created and instilled in her by her parents. She writes:

> The feminine desire to espouse the faith of those you love as I espoused my father's and then my mother's. I only swerved from each as my love changed. I swerved from admiration of my father's values to that of my mother's. But I am slowly finding my own. In my life today there is a freedom of emotion, a keenness of sensation, an explorative, adventurous attitude which is mine.
>
> (5:42)

Nin is splendidly aware that to individuate means to find one's own way through life, shedding our parental wounds.

Frequent Metamorphosis

To reinforce her newly found "adventurous attitude," throughout the subsequent years, Nin sought emotional freedom from the conflicts with her mother through analysis with her Jungian analyst, Martha Jaeger. In *Anaïs Nin and the Remaking of Self*, Diane Richard-Allerdyce writes that during therapy with Jaeger, Nin would "be able to see her mother's way of loving as sacrificing, and, as the model for Nin's own way of relating to others, a form of self-abnegation" (52–53). This is significant for the transformation of Nin's own feelings towards herself. "Once she distinguished between this role and her mother's bravery, she would be to some degree more able, consciously, to choose the traits to identify with, rejecting self-effacement and advocating women's embracing an active strength," writes Richard-Allerdyce (52–53).

While Nin grew her consciousness towards her maternal wound, she gained wisdom about what obstructs compassion for one's parents. Compassion for others who have wounded us, develops, according to Nin, through maturity and the ability to understand the power dynamics in relationships. In a passage filled with revelations, Nin writes:

> What blocks compassion often is an overestimation of the other's power. Power does not inspire sympathy. But often this power is imagined, such as the power we imagine held by the parents. True, at one time they had power over us, power of life or death, but this did not mean that they themselves did not have fears, doubts, pains, troubles, tragedies, and that at any moment they might need us desperately. Their strength was relative to our childish helplessness, but later they had a claim to our acceptance of their human fallibilities. In fact, I would say that compassion for our parents is the true sign of maturity.
>
> (5:188)

Moving through her own impassivity grants Nin the psychological possibility to also understand her parental wound, allowing her to embrace healing and a new sense of autonomy as a writer. Throughout her life, Nin turned to her writing to transform life's tragedies and uncertainties. Her persistent efforts to move through familial wounds (as a wounded daughter), by becoming intimate with, and then rewriting, the myths of her family, lead to healing the repressed pain encircling her family. In a diary entry written in the summer of 1957, Nin writes that through the guidance of her psychoanalyst, this time Dr. Bogner, she "began to remember moments of union with parents and brothers, moments of love, proofs of love. It was not as I had crystallized it, all pain and estrangement" (6:99). By tending to her traumatic memories, Nin gains access to a new emotional truth, nurturing a new understanding of her past.

By the end of the novelette, *Seduction of the Minotaur*, Lillian journeys homeward and embraces the "mystery" of a rebirth (95). She is traveling toward newly accepted parts of herself. The novelette's conclusion reads: "In silence, in mystery, a human being was formed, was exploded, was struck by other passing bodies, was burned, was deserted. And then it was born in the molten love of the one who cared" (136). Lillian has a new opportunity to participate in the feminine cosmic cycle of recreation that comes from tending to her maternal wound. She better understands how to love herself and others more authentically. By experiencing a new sensibility through her writing, Nin had what she called "frequent metamorphosis," suggesting that each creative act was akin to moving along a perpetual path towards self-realization (5:194). Through her writing, Nin seems to be able to have detected and understood the unnerving inner experiences that are brought about when creative ideas rupture. She let herself be transfigured by her courage to follow her imagination throughout her life.

In the Summer of 1954, shortly before her mother's death, she reflected on the vulnerabilities and anxieties to which the artist was subjected. She wondered what was needed for the artist to have the endurance and stamina to claim one's creative life. She was keenly aware that to be a writer required more than talent, as the creative life can take a psychological and physical toll on one's life. In impassioned prose she writes:

> It is true that there are elevations in art, in music, in writing which sustain us, help us to live. They transmute our sorrows into beauty. But it is also true that there are pitfalls from which art cannot save us, and then it becomes necessary to find an understanding of our human life, of our illness. I have found this understanding, this quest for healing and wholeness necessary to me and to others. The poets, I observed from my studies of the classical and modern romantics (whom we call neurotics), always end in catastrophe, in tragedy, illness, death. They were the victims of life rather than its conquerors. See the tragic life of Baudelaire, of Rimbaud, Verlaine, of Dylan Thomas. Only recently Virginia Woolf drowned herself. Rimbaud walked out of his poet's life and into oblivion.
>
> (5:170)

This passage captures a new sentiment to the notion that "writing was the way out" (Hinz, *A Woman Speaks* 225). Here Nin acknowledges that talent alone does not "sustain" the deep psychological process of transmuting sorrows "into beauty" in art (5:170). Woolf's room and economic independence did not save her. The autonomy of the female imagination depends, Nin knew, on the strength of one's interior world, a space that will help us hold our pain. Nin recognized, with greater clarity, that the artist must be able to survive the vicissitudes of the creative path. These new insights reflect Nin's maturity as a writer.

A Thousand Years of Womanhood

Figure 2.2 Anaïs Nin sitting by her printing press on MacDougal Street, New York, circa 1940s.

Throughout the 1960s and 1970s, as Nin tirelessly worked to edit and publish her diaries, she experienced high levels of stress and anxiety, including the tremendous angst that came with the critical reviews of her work. However, her reactions to the inner and outer pressures to succeed were better managed as she embodied a deeper sense of her autonomy as a writer. In essence, her efforts towards healing her maternal wound materialized into a renewed capacity for inner-guidance, strength and confidence.

Also, it is important to note that this is a time when Nin more fully surrounded herself by a community of brilliant women who were successful in their professions. In particular, Nin held a close friendship with the woman who introduced her to the literary world, Nona Balakian. In her unique position at the *New York Times*, working for "Belles Lettres," Nona was the first to review Volume 1 of Nin's expurgated diary, published in 1966. In Nona's collection of book reviews titled *Critical Encounters: Literary Views and Other Reviews*, published in 1991, she recalls her first encounter with Nin, writing: "the dazzlingly beautiful Anaïs Nin in her sixties, handing me the first volume of her *Diary* in manuscript, trembling to know if I thought it would at last bring her to the larger public's attention" (Balakian, *Critical Encounters* 12). Largely, by handing her first expurgated diary to Nona, Nin became known to the world. During the 1970s, Nona secured reviews for Nin's works, such as *Collages*, in *The New York Times*. Nin also developed a close friendship with Nona's sister Anna Balakian, an accomplished professor of French and comparative literature at New York University, who reviewed Volume 4 of Nin's diary for the *New York Times*. In the opening of her review, Anna Balakian writes in persuasive prose:

> Anaïs Nin is one of the most extraordinary and unconventional writers of this century. Her vast diary, which encompasses some 50 years of human relationships, resembles no other in the history of letters, and as a novelist she has been distinctly catalytic
>
> (Balakian, "The Diary of Anaïs Nin")

Another important friendship I discovered was the one Nin developed with artist Judy Chicago, famous for creating the powerful feminist installation artwork "The Dinner Table." In their conversation about women and creativity in 1972, Chicago introduces Nin as her "friend and aesthetic mother" (KPFA, "Voices of Independence"). Nin did more than mother the male literati of her time; she also came to be a symbolic mother to countless female artists of future generations, including my own.

In one of the final passages of Volume 6 of her diary, which is the last volume that she prepared for publication in 1976, the year before she died, Nin reflects on the type of artist she has become: one who has lived outside of the social roles and creative expectations imposed by patriarchal rules. She writes: "I will no longer be vulnerable to the old cliche that I am only interested in the personal" (6:400). Nin, it seems, finally and firmly, believed in her voice and in the archetypal qualities that her work embodies. As if to demystify the impulse of her creative life, she reflects on the meaning of her work:

> At the end of this diary I feel I have accomplished what I hoped to accomplish: to reveal how personal errors influence the whole of history and that our real objective is to create a human being who will not go to war.
>
> (6:399–400)

Nin's lifelong conviction as an artist was to explore, and depict, the formation of an individual who could understand her own psychological and spiritual temperaments, and who had the courage to pursue her creative endeavors, alone, again and again. Embodying a poetic sensibility, Nin felt it was her "destiny to live the drama of feeling and imagination, reality and unreality, the drama without guns, dynamite, explosions" (6:400). Her references to war remind us that she valued the inner peace brought forth by the self-realization embedded in the creative process. Creativity, Nin knew, required courage. To this, she writes: "My span may seem smaller, but it is really larger because it covers all the obscure routes of the soul and body seeking truth, seeking the antiserum against hate and war, never receiving medals for its courage" (6:400). Her work shows us the life of a female writer who understood that we must be able and willing to travel "the obscure routes of the soul and body seeking truth" – to seek our truths, and then be willing to release those truths out into the world.

Deepened consciousness, according to Nin, could be the "antiserum" needed in society to fight "hate and war." Nin was committed to the creative process and the visions that were within her own being that held immense archetypal resonances. She remained unrequitedly committed to her art, not to receive "medals for courage," but because she knew she needed her art to survive (6:400). Her bravery undergirds instead the inner resolution that it takes to be an embodied artist, discovering new symbols, a feminine orientation, and patterns and myths from which to build a fresh vision of the world, again and again. Intimacy with self, and the capacity to be vulnerable through each creative act, requires perpetual courage. It is interesting to note that the word courage is derived from the Latin word *cor*, meaning heart (Etymonline). In the same way that courage is etymologically connected to the body, so was Nin's search for self-actualization.

Ultimately, toward the end of her life, Nin maintained a stronger conviction of herself as a writer, including her "artistic values," which she set out to create in the first volume of her expurgated diary, in 1932

(1:103). Following the long and illustrious arc of her life, in the conclusion of volume 6 of the diary, she reflects on the meaning behind her life's work. The final sentence reads with great resolution: "It is my thousand years of womanhood I am recording, a thousand women. It would be simpler, shorter, swifter not to seek this deepening perspective to my life and lose myself in the simple world of war, hunger, death" (6:400). Nin viewed her life as dynamic and through a multitude of archetypes. She also valued the mythmaking possibilities of the human mind. This wisdom guided her both toward and past thresholds, involving twists and turns in her life.

No other twentieth-century writer has been so intent on the value of staying close, with intentional focus on her own imagination and psyche. Her life and work offer us an intimate and poetic portrait of the life of the steadfast artist who was able to endure the tribulations of a deeply creative life. Throughout her writing in the diary, which she kept for over sixty years, she captures the powerful and intimate encounter between the artist and her inner and outer world. In this regard, Nin was in a state of continual flow with the interior and exterior experiences of her life, which helped her create a lasting connection to others. I do not suggest "flow" to mean an unrelenting state of harmony, but rather that Nin took responsibility for her own creative life, continuously willing to embrace the mysteries brought forth throughout psychic movements prompted by creativity. She strongly valued the role of the creative process as self-expression and as the path towards consciousness of her deepest self. Nin's creative credo provides ways to think about our inner lives, even when it is difficult to see beauty and possibilities to grow into our creative potential as women.

In her literary works, we find a matrilineal literary heritage that in the words of Virginia Woolf, we receive from the "writers that have gone through a great deal to free us .... The writers of the next generation may inherit from them a whole state of mind, a mind no longer rippled, evasive, divided" (Woolf 14). We inherit, from Nin, an example of a daring writer who was propelled by her inner wisdom and the need to be free to travel her own "obscure routes of the soul," roads towards individuation. Nin's life reveals the possibilities of embracing the ever-unfolding feminine wisdom that is uniquely one's own to claim, regardless of perceived powerlessness. Nin, it is my belief, succeeded in re-mapping the harmful experiences from her past, and the beauty of her creative life, including inner and outer experiences and narratives that shaped her. She did it one creative act at a time. She left us a body of work that shows a steep arc of growth, and proof of a firm commitment to the creative life of an artist.

A Mother's Biography

To Nin's deep regret, the moment of a mother sharing the intimate details of her life with her daughter never did materialize for Rosa and Nin. Rosa never called on her daughter to be her vindex, "a protector, a defender, someone who demands compensation for reputational damage, the person who, in a word, repairs ..." (Léger 31). This means that the biographical sketch Nin wrote at twelve years old of her mother's singing talents (referenced in the introduction of this chapter) would be the closest biographical depiction she would ever write about her own mother.

Yet, as this note I came upon in her unexpurgated papers reveals, Nin did try. Nin writes the tender words describing her attempt to learn more about her mother's life story, so that she could write the "story of her life":

> I was born ...
>   The last day I spent with my mother I tried to persuade her to dictate the story of her life. I wrote these words: I am born ... and waited. But she made fun of this idea ... and I desisted.
>   She died Wednesday August 3, 1954 at approximately 5 o'clock p.m.
>   (Anaïs Nin Papers)

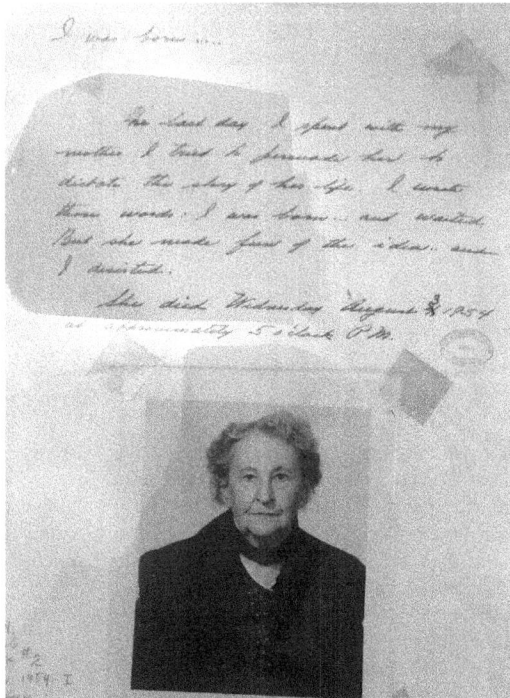

Figure 2.3 A page from the archives of Anaïs Nin, including a picture of her mother, Rosa Culmell Vaurigaud, 1954.

Journeying toward the "Obscure Routes of the Soul and Body Seeking Truth"

On January 14, 1977, Nin took her last breath at Cedars-Sinai Medical Center in Los Angeles, just one month before turning 74. She died of cervical cancer. By mere coincidence, I have met the nurse, Cheryle Van Scoy, with whom Nin's doctor consulted to assist him in setting up a home hospice for Nin. He asked Cheryle, who had been in the role of prioritizing comfort and quality of life for the terminally ill for years, to meet with Nin to assess her needs. Cheryle was left in charge of finding the right nurses to train to tend to Nin during her final days.[15] Cheryle had witnessed people lay in the liminality between life and death countless times before. She had experienced the multitude of ways the physicality of the transitioning body relates to the individual's suffering. In a personal interview with Cheryle in the summer of 2024, she described to me her experience of being in Nin's presence as being unlike any other she had ever experienced. Upon entering the room, as Nin lay still and delicate on an oversized hospital bed, Cheryle was immediately met with Nin's "luminous" aura. As they softly spoke about Nin going home, Nin's frail body was "more soul than physical body," as she had "a lightness of being while her body was slipping away." What came to mind for Cheryle as she shared this "gift of an experience" with me was C. G. Jung's notion that throughout life, as we move toward aging, instead of the ego expanding, it's about growing the soul. Nin, on her hospital bed, Cheryle shared, exuded the impression of being "a person who could surrender to what awaited her." Her experience of Nin's lightness of being was that of being in the presence of someone who "was highly individuated."

I have come to understand this image of a luminous and ethereal Anaïs Nin, at the end of her life, to reflect the beauty and force of the Great Mother within her. The image of Nin enveloped in luminosity, taking her final breaths, further suggests that her steadfast search and ability, throughout her life, was to journey "the obscure routes of the soul and body seeking truths" (6:400). Indeed, her soul's motivation *was* toward individuation, while on earth, in ultimate preparation for death.

Notes

1 Citations in this format are from *The Diary of Anaïs Nin*, volumes 1–6, giving the volume number before the colon and page number(s) after it. Citations beginning "ED" (followed by the volume number) refer to *The Early Diary of Anaïs Nin* (although volume 1 of that series, *Linotte*, is cited under its own title).
2 I have written about Nin's relationship with her father in *Anaïs Nin: A Myth of Her Own*. Other scholars have written about Nin's male-centric world. See Bettina Knapp's *Anaïs Nin* and Evelyn Hinz's *The Mirror and the Garden: Realism and Reality in the Writings of Anaïs Nin*.
3 Rosa died on August 3, 1954 in California. She was 82 and was buried in Havana, Cuba, beside her father (5:177).
4 I write extensively of Nin's myth-making process in my work *Anaïs Nin: A Myth of Her Own*.
5 Joaquin went by Joaquin Nin-Culmell to distinguish himself from his father.

6 In the early diaries, Nin references her husband as Hugh. In the expurgated diaries, Hugh's artistic name became Hugo.

7 Nin claimed that it was the "vivacious literary life of Paris" that gave her the courage and maturity to creatively engage with her wounds (Hinz, *A Woman Speaks* 224).

8 It is important to point out a curiosity: the next month after this entry, Nin would write the incest narrative chronicled in the unexpurgated diary *Incest: From a 'Journal of Love,'* posthumously published in 1992. In *Anaïs Nin: A Myth of Her Own,* I analyze the use of incest as a metaphor for the incessant hold that patriarchal structures, as represented in her long-time traumatic events around her father, had on her psyche.

9 The reflection around this pregnancy in Nin's expurgated diary suggests it is a stillbirth. However, in the unexpurgated diary this reads like an abortion. Diane Richard-Allerdyce and biographer Deirdre Bair discuss the pregnancy in detail in their respective books.

10 Thus, writing as a metaphorical "way out" is one of Nin's expressions of the development of consciousness that is the individuation path (Hinz, *A Woman Speaks* 225). Nin dedicated her life to forging and creating her freedom and creative potential as a writer. She knew that paying heed to the creative impulse was the way towards making evident her deepest feelings about life. She never, that I am aware of, suggested that there was an ultimate "way out," nor did she believe that writing was the way out for everyone.

11 I analyze this topic in "The Literary Credo of a Diarist and Noveletteist as Traced in *Incest: From a Journal of Love* and *Winter of Artifice,*" in *Anaïs Nin: A Myth of Her Own.*

12 See Irigaray's work in *The Way of Love* and Hélène Cixous's work in "The Laugh of the Medusa."

13 In April 1947 Nin writes in her diary about having to leave the United States to re-enter as a permanent resident, and made plans to go to Mexico. This is also around the time when she accepted an invitation to drive west to California with Rupert Pole in his Ford Model A. On the trip from New York to Los Angeles, Nin and Pole stop in to see D. H. Lawrence's widow Frieda Lawrence in New Mexico. This is an emotional visit. When Frieda offers Nin the possibility of staying in the cottage where the Lawrences first lived upon moving to New Mexico, Nin declines: "I was reluctant to go into the past of my literary loves as of my human ones. I was curious about tomorrow, about what new places we were going to discover" (4:196, 206). In this freedom of movement through her own intuition, Nin creates Lillian, who finds herself in Mexico, experiencing awakened and deepened consciousness.

14 Citations of "Anaïs Nin Papers" refer to the archives held at UCLA Special Collections.

15 Nin did not make it home to hospice. She died in the hospital shortly after her meeting with Cheryle.

References

Bair, Deirdre. *Anaïs Nin: A Biography.* New York. G. P. Putnam's Sons. 1995.

Balakian, Anna. "The Diary of Anaïs Nin." New York Times. January 16, 1972.

Balakian, Nona. *Critical Encounters: Literary Views and Other Reviews.* New York. Ashold Press. 1991.

Benstock, Shari. *Women of the Left Bank: Paris 1900–1940.* Austin. University of Texas Press, 1986.

Cor. Courage. Retrieved from www.etymonline.com/search?q=courage. Accessed March 2024.

Cusk, Rachel. "Annie Ernaux Has Broken Every Taboo of What Women are Allowed to Write." *New York Times Magazine.* March, 2023.

Ferrante, Elena. *In the Margins: On the Pleasures of Reading and Writing*. London. Europa Editions. 2022.

Fitch, Noël Riley. *The Erotic Life of Anaïs Nin*. New York. Little Brown and Company. 1993.

Gray, Frances. *Jung, Irigaray, Individuation: Philosophy, Analytical Psychology, and the Question of the Feminine*. London. Routledge. 2019.

Hinz, Evelyn J. *A Woman Speaks: The Lectures, Seminars, and Interviews of Anaïs Nin*. Chicago. The Swallow Press. 1975.

Hinz, Evelyn J. *The Mirror and the Garden: Realism and Reality in the Writings of Anais Nin*. New York. Harcourt Brace Jovanovich. 1973.

Knapp, Bettina. *Anaïs Nin*. New York. Frederick Ungar Publishing. 1978.

KPFA. "Voices of Independence – Judy Chicago & Anais Nin in Conversation." Recorded in 1972. Broadcast July 4, 2018. Retrieved from https://kpfa.org/episode/voices-of-independence-judy-chicago-anais-nin-in-conversation.

Lawrence, D. H. "A Propos of 'Lady Chatterley's Lover'." *Lady Chatterley's Lover*. New York. Penguin Books. 2006.

Léger, Natalie. *The White Dress*. London. Les Fugitives. 2018.

McEville, Wayne. *Seduction of the Minotaur*. Ohio. The Swallow Press. 1961.

Nalbantian, Suzanne. "Nin, Borges and Paz: Labyrinthine Passageways of Mind and Language." *Memory in Literature: From Rousseau to Neuroscience*. New York: Palgrave Macmillan. 2003.

Nin, Anaïs. *Collages*. Chicago. The Swallow Press. 1992.

Nin, Anaïs. *D. H. Lawrence: An Unprofessional Study*. Chicago. The Swallow Press. 1964.

Nin, Anaïs. *The Diary of Anaïs Nin Volume 1 (1931–1934)*. New York. Harvest. 1966.

Nin, Anaïs. *The Diary of Anaïs Nin Volume 2 (1934–1939)*. New York. Harvest. 1967.

Nin, Anaïs. *The Diary of Anaïs Nin Volume 3 (1939–1944)*. New York. Harvest. 1969.

Nin, Anaïs. *The Diary of Anaïs Nin Volume 4 (1944–1947)*. New York. Harvest. 1971.

Nin, Anaïs. *The Diary of Anaïs Nin Volume 5 (1947–1955)*. New York. Harvest. 1974.

Nin, Anaïs. *The Diary of Anaïs Nin Volume 6 (1955–1966)*. New York. Harvest. 1976.

Nin, Anaïs. *The Early Diary of Anaïs Nin Volume 2 (1920–1923)*. San Diego. Harcourt Brace & Co. 1983.

Nin, Anaïs. *The Early Diary of Anaïs Nin Volume 3 (1923–1927)*. San Diego. Harcourt Brace & Co. 1983.

Nin, Anaïs. *The Early Diary of Anaïs Nin Volume 4 (1927–1931)*. San Diego. Harcourt Brace & Co. 1985.

Nin, Anaïs. *The Four Chambered Heart*. Athens. Swallow Press. 1959.

Nin, Anaïs. "Hejda." *Under a Glass Bell and Other Stories*. Denver. Swallow Press. 1961.

Nin, Anaïs. *House of Incest*. Athens. Swallow Press. 1958.

Nin, Anaïs. *Linotte: The Early Diary of Anaïs Nin Volume 1 (1914–1920)*. New York. Harvest. 1978.

Nin, Anaïs. *The Novel of the Future*. New York. Collier Books. 1968.

Nin, Anaïs. *Seduction of the Minotaur*. Ohio. The Swallow Press. 1961.

Nin-Culmell, Joaquin. "Growing Up with Anaïs Nin, Studying with De Falla, Composing in the Spanish Tradition: Interviews Conducted by Caroline Crawford." 2002. Retrieved from https://digicoll.lib.berkeley.edu/record/218220?v=pdf.

Oropeza, Clara. *Anaïs Nin: A Myth of Her Own*. Abingdon. Routledge. 2018.

Richard-Allerdyce, Diane. *Anaïs Nin and the Remaking of Self, Gender, Modernism, and Narrative Identity*. Dekalb. Northern Illinois University Press. 1998.

Spencer, Sharon. *Collage of Dreams: Writings of Anaïs Nin*. Chicago. The Swallow Press. 1977.

Woolf, Virginia. *A Room of One's Own*. London. Hogarth Press. 1929.

Chapter 3

The Individuation Path of a Mexican Woman: *Fuerte y Desahogada* (Strong and Undrowned)

(Mexico and the United States)

There is no greater agony than bearing an untold story inside of you.[1]

(Zora Neale Hurston 176)

In 1965, a Mexican woman insisted on an education for her daughters. Already in possession of a US green card, she orchestrated the details of emigrating with her husband and two young daughters (one daughter, age two, and the other, age five) from Nogales Sonora, Mexico to Tucson, Arizona. She alone secured housing, found a job for her husband, and enrolled her eldest daughter in school. She alone made the fateful decision to set a path for her daughters' freedom, one that would be away from the life-defining poverty she had lived. Her own life experiences and encoded messages that she conceded to would teach her daughters the dominant rules and expectations of women in a patriarchal world. There was an unspoken understanding of the battles waged by patriarchy upon her person and psyche, which later revealed what she was made to keep hidden – her inner strengths. That woman is my mother. Her individuation story told here involves the de-shaming of a feminine experience, while finding her footing in life.

Her name, Maria Ramona Isabel (1939–), personifies a connection to her matrilineal: her maternal grandmother, Maria Acosta; her paternal grandmother, Ramona Badilla; and her mother, Isabel Quijada.

My mother was familiar with the sacrifices of the migrant dream. It began twenty-two years earlier, in 1943, on a hot Sonoran summer day, when Ramona, or Maye as she was called, and her family of seven siblings, along with her parents, a *vaquero* and a homemaker, left Saric, Sonora, Mexico shrouded in the paradox of hope and darkness. That somber journey characterized the unpredictability of their fate, palpable in the warm wind blowing on their backs, while they rode in the back of a 1939 pickup truck driven by her father's brother, *Tio* Diego. They arrived in Nogales, Sonora, Mexico, where they settled temporarily until the next opportunity could be seized to continue their migration into the United States. In Nogales, Sonora, the Martinez clan rented a one room studio with a sparsely paved floor. At night, from their sleeping cots, one could gaze toward the ceiling and see strips of the night sky through the ceiling cracks. My mother was four years old at the time, the youngest daughter of eight surviving children. By the

DOI: 10.4324/9781003255857-3

time my mother made it into the world, her own mother was by now familiar with the tragedies of child mortality, as she had lost four infant children. After my mother was born, two more children would not survive the perils of poverty. The abject poverty left an emotional scar on her for the rest of her life.

Within weeks of their arrival in Nogales, her father, a clean-shaven young man of 39, left the family to make the 500-mile trek to New Mexico to work as a vaquero on a white man's ranch. He remained sequestered there for several years, and when he finally returned, his prolonged absence was apparent by his appearance. His long, unkept beard and shoulder-length hair made him unrecognizable to his children. The part of him that was still familiar was his struggle with alcoholism.

During his absence, Isabel, my mother's mother, solidified her role as the matriarch of the family. However, the kind of matriarch she would become, and the demands she would put on her children, were set by the social-economic standards of their time. They were a close-knit family, so it was unspoken that everyone's duty, no matter age or gender, was for the survival of the family. As for my grandmother, even though she was overwhelmed by her own trauma and her own maternal wound, she understood the code of a mother's instinctual need to dedicate her life to the basic survival of her children. There would be no time to process her own grief, or little time left for mothering them emotionally, much less steering them through life. Instead, parental love was expressed through having basic material needs met. The lack of a primal maternal bond and the accompanying economic poverty of her childhood made it difficult for my mother to shape a secure understanding and feeling of love, safety, self-confidence, and her womanhood. Having not received emotional validation from either parent, she would be unable to provide it for her daughters.

My Mother's Mother

On May 6, 1907, my grandmother, Isabel Quijada, was born into a humble family in Saric, Sonora. Her father was a talented carpenter and her mother, a homemaker. As a child she was thoughtful and affectionate. Isabel possessed a captivating physical appearance. As a young woman, she wore her dark, oak-colored hair short, and with an elegant natural wave. Her dark brown almond shaped eyes had a gaze of wonder, and her lips, with a soft smile with a beauty mark above her top lip. Growing up, she spent her childhood surrounded by red earth, which granted her a sacred connection to it as a birthright. The earth that cradled her, also gave her solid Mexican indigenous roots. These home roots would be portable as they would cling to her immigrant feet and help carry her to all the places that she would eventually live. These roots would become the spiritual ground of her inner self and become her greatest silent strength. She would forsake "home" to keep climbing, raising her family above a life of the poverty that she lived.

In 1928 Isabel met Guillermo, my grandfather, in Saric, Sonora, Mexico. It was the same year that Isabel's mother became terminally ill at 48 years old and passed away. Although her mother was preoccupied with the physical survival of her family, she would pass onto her daughter a determined spirit. My great-grandmother also cultivated in my grandmother the talents of a seamstress and prepared her for other life skills for fulfilling the role of wife and mother. Even in the days before her mother slipped into unconsciousness, my great-grandmother, in a prolepsis manner, advised Isabel that if Guillermo was interested in marrying her, she should accept his proposal. Soon after-wards, Isabel, at 21 years old, was left motherless. Her mother's last words of wisdom were that, within society, at the time, a man's interest in a woman should be heeded, and her own desires and dreams set aside, forgotten.

My mother grew up in a family where the father came first, and sons were more valued than daughters. Her emotional bond to my grandmother was ambivalent since the basic survival of the family was the most important thing. This emotional distance is what shaped my mother's own maternal wound. In those days, my grandmother sought a luminous center inhabited by prayer. My grandmother would include her youngest daughter of the three (the other two daughters were already adults living their own lives) in the daily community gathering of women to pray the rosary to La Virgen de Guadalupe. Through her contemplative practice, my grandmother would set down her own quotidian struggles at the Virgin's altar. It was there, in the stillness beneath the neighbor's ivy-covered porch, where a simple altar sat on a white wrought iron table. It is there where red votive candles burned in tin cans for La Virgen, and where my mother, just a child, joined the group of women to pray to their Goddess. Women and girls of cross generations lit candles to celebrate a protected mother who mirrored the radiance of a Goddess and who invited them to cultivate self-knowledge. As the women turned inward, they were met with the inner "other" of which their own lives were to strive for: motherhood, sacrifice and honor. This is where my mother was initiated into the ways of spirituality and womanhood. During these early years, La Virgen de Guadalupe became the symbolic mother and role model of womanhood. This was a pivotal path for my mother's individuation, and from where to tell my mother's story. Her story is about the complex ways that a cultural narrative such as that of La Virgen de Guadalupe, who represents the ultimate revered spiritual, archetype of motherhood, loyalty and self-sacrifice, pervaded her psychic life, and how she sought to overcome the cruel and difficult realities for women during that time. Centered in my mother's life was a tension about what was missing from the Vir-gen's narrative: on how to embrace motherhood in nature as a woman. That being said, how does a woman become the all-giving mother amid her own sexuality, sensuality and desire in order to find true love? How do women become young mothers while also remaining chaste, effervescent and true to themselves? In Mex-ican, patriarchal society, virginity is venerated more than motherhood. The Virgen de Guadalupe archetype was a way for my mother to become acquainted with the depths of her own struggles. As a woman, she suffered the perils in a culture that celebrated motherhood in relationship to the ultimate mother, but condemned motherhood in parts of nature.

Women's Rights in 1940s Mexico

In the 1940s, women's rights in Mexico had developed momentum from the first feminist congress held in 1915 (Pablos 93). Working-and-middle-class women were no longer confined to the home as some revolutionary leaders were aware of the importance of improving the quality of life for women. In her book *Women in Mexico: A Past Unveiled*, Julia Tuñón Pablos points out that since Emiliano Zapata's demands in 1917 were for land and "respect for the autonomy of the pueblos," women too held military rank in his army (92). At the same time, there were other men in powerful positions beginning to advocate for women's rights. One of those was Salvador Alvarado, the governor of Yucatán, from 1915–1919. He rightly proclaimed, "until we raise women up it will be impossible for us to serve [our] country" (Pablos 94). The advocacy and organization by the various women's groups of the time, such as Club Femenil Amigas del Pueblo, and Hijas de Cuauhtémoc, lead to the new Constitution of 1917, giving "women legal equality, with the same rights and duties as men, including the legal right to sign contracts and manage their own business and property" (96). In 1923, Gabriela Mistral, Chilean poet and educator, speaks to women in Mexico City and encourages them to "[a]sk for your child a bright, clean school … demand collaboration in certain laws; make them erase the shame of the illegitimate child, and do not permit them to let this child be born and live as an outcast, in the midst of other happy children" (150). Mistral empowers women to be courageous in the face of the injustices they, along with their children, faced.

While there were new laws that were supposed to foster improvement to gender equality, women were still relegated to working in the textile, garment, *maquiladoras*, food, agricultural industries, where gender equity was non-existent (108). These rights did not offer relief from the oppression of low wages. Nor was there any lack of free will, a pivotal requisite to uplifting the lives of the working-class women, including the lives of my grandmother and her three daughters. Women were still expected to rely on a husband to validate their own existence, given that they would need their husband's consent to work or do anything outside the home. Women would not be given suffrage until 1953.

The fight for suffrage was not on the minds of my grandmother or her daughters. Instead, material survival took up all their hours of the day. Their lives were impacted by the *machismo* and the embedded patriarchal constraints of the Mexican society that relegated women as second-class citizens. While women throughout Mexican society lived under these limits, as inscribed from their gender, women found inventive ways to move past these limits to help their family survive. Julia Tuñón Pablos writes:

> Sexism is neither a conspiracy of one sex against the other nor a biological fact. It is a *social system*. Faced with this system, women had collectively become aware that they deserved the best possible world, and that this world is worth struggling for.
>
> (115)

But how could women set themselves free in a society that was engineered against them? By the time women got the right to vote in Mexico, in 1953, my mother and her family had emigrated to Red Rock, Arizona.[2] During that time, her father worked for a different white rancher, who, after a year of employment, offered to sponsor the entire Martinez family for the permanent residency. Finally, for the first time in years, the Martinez clan would reunite. This time, in the United States.

Bridging the Personal with the Cultural Image of the All Giving Mother: La Virgen de Guadalupe

At the age of 16, Ramona was sent away by her family to live and work in Los Angeles. It was during this time that La Virgen de Guadalupe became

Figure 3.1 Ramona Martinez, circa 1954.

her confidante. Her first job was in downtown Los Angeles, working in the garment industry sewing buttons onto women's blouses. She was paid a piece rate of 25 cents per blouse. There, she faced a demand of completing as many products as possible in a day, which led to various accidents, like nearly sewing buttons through her own fingers. On many occasions, she landed in the doctor's office, located down the street from the factory. Initially, this began as a part-time job she worked at after school. However, as economic demands increased, the intensified need to work full-time meant leaving her education behind. My mother's own immigrant story is one of struggle to get an education amid securing basic needs. She would never return to school. Her dreams to study either cosmetology or psychology would never be realized. She would instead live out her educational dream vicariously through her daughters. While living in Los Angeles, Ramona had her eldest sister's support. The two sisters did not grow up in the same household for much of their lives mainly because of the nine-year age difference. This meant they had not cultivated a bond between two sisters with intertwined lives. This closeness would come later, but at the time, there was a palpable estrangement between the two sisters.

Homesick and lonely, my mother, through silent prayers, then turned to La Virgen de Guadalupe for guidance in matters about sexuality and protection in the way that a woman, who lived away from her family, was told to do. "*Fue como una madre para mi*" ("She was like a mother to me"), is how my mother described her relationship with La Virgen. "*Simpre fue mi virgencita*" ("She was always my *virgencita*") (Martinez). One of the guiding messages that this mother taught women of my mother's generation was that they needed to protect their chastity until marriage in order to be an honorable and respected woman. My mother, like the women of her time, was uneducated in family planning and was reared to believe that by summoning the Virgen's faith into this matter, she would, one day, marry a virgin in the Catholic Church with "*la virgencita como mi testigo*" ("with the virgin mother as my witness") (Martinez). My mother's own coming of age was mapped out for her within this cultural and social backdrop of motherhood.

The Virgen's story is not only the tale of a miracle that speaks about mystery and motherhood, but also the story about the interaction between the human and the divine grounded in gender constructs. It is a story that intertwines womanhood and motherhood as the most significant narrative of my mother's individuation. My mother's entire life had been aligned for her to encounter the mother goddess. The goddess demanded that Ramona align her own experiences with this embodiment of the feminine. As James Hillman in *Re-Visioning Psychology* reminds us, the psychologizing process of asking questions of our lives involves knowing what goddess we align with. Hillman writes:

> The questions of why things are as they are, how they came about, and
> how to settle them – even those of what is going on and what it means –

find ultimate issue in revelation of the particular archetypal persona at work in the event. Once we know at whose altar the question belongs, then we know better the manner of proceeding.

(139)

My mother's central and complex questions about womanhood and motherhood were placed at the altar of La Virgen de Guadalupe. She believed that it was her right as a woman to love her and entrust her with her life's orientation. As this goddess was infused with vital personal and cultural meaning, and the archetypal energy tapped into her psyche, La Virgen de Guadalupe also held the tensions centered within my mother's individuation story – that being, how to be a mother in a society that only sees women in one state: the ideal mother.

The Mother Goddess

According to Stafford Poole's research in *Our Lady of Guadalupe: The Origins and Sources of a Mexican National Symbol, 1531–1797*, the apparition version that we know of today was first documented in 1649 by Luis Laso de la Vega, a priest. The account was found in the *Nican Mopohua* (written in Nahuatl) (Poole 26). On December 12, 1531 (ten years following the conquest of Mexico) Juan Diego was walking along the hill of Tepeyac, when he heard the song of birds on his path. Then he heard himself being called "to the top of the hill by a woman's voice" (26). Once on the hilltop, "he saw a resplendent vision of a woman who identified herself as the Virgen, 'the other of the great true deity God, the giver of life, the creator of people, the lord of the universe, possessor of heaven and earth'" (26). In a tender manner, she instructed him to go to the bishop of Mexico and request that a church be built for her on the hilltop. Initially, the bishop did not believe Juan Diego. He returned to the apparition site and asked the Virgen for a more tangible sign of her vision to prove it to the disbelieving bishop. In turn, she instructed Juan Diego to return to the hill to find "'every kind of precious Spanish flower' in a place where flowers did not grow ..." (27).[3] He brought the flowers inside his *tilma*. [4] According to her instructions, Diego would only open his cloak in the bishop's presence. What lay in the folds of the cloak were the proof needed: "When he unfolded his *tilma*, the flowers fell to the floor, and printed on the cloak was the image of the Virgin" (28). Subsequently, plans to construct the chapel at Tepeyac were immediately put into motion.

Myths are guides that impart sacred knowledge about the world. Myths allow depth into our own thinking and feeling about our ancestors and our own lives. In La Virgen de Guadalupe's myth, upon a closer look at her iconographic representation in the one and only way that she is represented, puts us into contact with her indigenous roots. In *Homage La Diosa de las Americas (The Goddess of the America): Writings on the Virgin of Guadalupe*, Ana

Castillo draws attention to the richness of the Nahua symbolism and meaning in her imagery. For example, La Virgen stands tranquil, with hands in prayer position. She wears a blue-green mantel, like a rebozo used by Indian women, around her delicate body, with the colors of the quetzal – the highland bird whose name means precious or sacred in several Mesoamerican languages (XX). She stands tall against a gold backdrop. Castillo reminds us, that "*La Virgen* wears the fertility sash, She is *en cinta*, pregnant, but the little symbol of the forthcoming child that dangles below it is the nagvioli flower, which represented Hitzilopochtli, the great, ferocious sun god of the Aztec" (XIX). At the base of her feet is a crescent moon, relating to her connection as the goddess of the night, and her footing is embraced by a child. This child has been interpreted as the forthcoming child, or the angel that is delivering her to motherhood (XX). The soft gaze in her downcast eyes is an expression of her humility and compassion. This "mysterious smile has been likened to the sacred version of Da Vinci's Mona Lisa ..." (XX).

For the Mexi-Amerindians, she was recognized as the mother goddess Tonantzin "our Mother" (Castillo xvii). Castillo reminds us of the depths and meaning she holds for indigenous peoples. She identified herself to Juan Diego in the following ways that are all immediately recognizable in the Aztec religion, as they are the five names given to the Supreme God of the Nahua people:

Inninantzin in huelneli Teotl Dios: Mother of the True God.
Inninantzin inipalnemohuani: Mother of the Giver of Life.
Inninantzin in Teyocoyani: Mother of the Inventor of Humanity.
Inninantzin in Tloque Nahaque: Mother of the Lord of Near and Far (this in fact is the name of the omnipotent, invisible Supreme Creator known to the pre-Conquest Mexicans).
Inninantzin in Ilhicahua in Tlalticpaque: Mother of (the Lord of) Heaven and Earth.

(XVII)

This context is essential to understanding the impacts of the tensions instilled during colonization on the Mexican psyche.

Moreover, by re-membering La Virgen's indigenous roots, we rediscover Her relation to a more complex feminine. Gloria Anzaldúa in *Borderlands La Frontera: The New Mestiza*, recounts that the "male-dominated Aztec-Mexica culture drove the powerful female deities underground by giving them monstrous attributes and by substituting male deities in their place, thus splitting the female self and the female deities" (49). This practice led to dividing "her who had been complete, who possessed both upper (light) and underworld (dark) aspects. Coatlicue, the Serpent goddess [of creativity and destruction], and her more sinister aspects, Tlazolteotl and Cihuacoatl, were 'darkened' and disempowered much in the same manner as the Indian Kali" (49).

The disempowering of the Goddess continued: "the Spaniards and their Church continued to split Tonantsi/Guadalupe. They desexed Guadalupe, taking Coatlalopeu, the serpent/sexuality, out of her" (50). This was a practice to disempower the feminine in the collective, which the colonial power perpetuated. The split that results in a one-dimensional depiction of the feminine is a way of disempowering the feminine in all of her complexities, and thus of her humanity.

In the transformation of 1531, while she is linked to the other Nahua goddesses, La Virgen de Guadalupe's main attribute is that of chaste virgin and protective mother with a womb. Yet with no apparent sexuality, she is without the dual force of life and death. This is the version that my mother and the women of her generation came to understand as their Goddess and role model of womanhood.

Yet, like all myths, La Virgen de Guadalupe would symbolize different things to different groups and individuals. As Poole writes:

> For Hidalgo and his ragtag army of Indians bent on revenge for centuries of oppression, as for Emiliano Zapata's *sureños* fighting for land and liberty, Guadalupe symbolized liberation and native rights. For others, Guadalupe has had various meanings: indigenism, religious syncretism, respect for cultural autonomy, the struggle for human dignity, or, conversely, submission and subjugation, whether of Indians or women. Most frequently, Guadalupe is associated with *mexicanida*.
>
> (4)

It is important to point out the irony of men carrying the Virgen's banner to fight for freedom: women are battling for their own freedom from the patriarchal constructs that they uphold and from which the men benefit.

For many women of my mother's generation, a relationship with La Virgen de Guadalupe is central to their cultural-religious identity. In her essay "Guadalupe: The Feminine Face of God," Jeanette Rodriguez considers the ways some Mexican women experience La Virgen. Rodriguez writes about the meaning that is ascribed to Her when women are in a relationship with Her in their daily life. Rodriguez interviews women who self-identify as being in "close relationship with the Virgen":

> In the interviews with the women in my study, we have seen how they take their troubles to Our Lady of Guadalupe because they experience her as being compassionate and responsive to their needs, in a way which, if present, nevertheless has not been identified in their relationship to God. She will understand them better than the male face of God because she too is female and a mother ... Again and again, the women in my study found that in encountering and being in the presence of Our Lady of Guadalupe, they regained their sense of self in an accepting and empowering relationship.
>
> (Rodriguez 29)

Generally, for women of my mother's generation, Guadalupe's role as goddess naturally brings her into association with an ability to confide in a "female and a mother" who takes on the guise of a feminine template for women. Like the women in Rodriguez's study, my mother experiences La Virgen de Guadalupe as the ideal feminine representation of the giver of life, of protection and of sacrifice. Yet, for my mother, being in relationship with this symbolic mother archetype, while coming into her own womanhood, began to pose a challenge. The challenge being that as a supreme image of womanhood, La Virgen de Guadalupe left no space for a woman's own biology, and thus humanity. Regarding Her absent sensuality, Ramona never questioned it. Nor did she ever openly consider whether the goddess of procreation was ever associated with anything else other than childbearing or the biological creation of children.

When considering Guadalupe's role in the collective imagination, it is interesting to note that she plays a prominent role as the mother goddess archetype in the lyrics of the popular Mexican folk songs, *corridos*, a musical form popular in Mexico which encompasses three genres: epic, lyric and narrative (Herrera-Sobek xiii). In her book *The Mexican Corrido: A Feminist Analysis*, María Herrera-Sobek looks at the way that:

> [t]he Virgin of Guadalupe generally appears as a protector for men in the corrido's mythic structure. In some songs, she is an important component at the beginning of the hero's adventure as it was structured by Joseph Campbell in *The Hero with a Thousand Faces* (1973).
>
> (48)

In the narratives, once the hero hears and heeds the call to adventure, Guadalupe is the protagonist's "helper" (48). She protects, aides and supports them in their own endeavors. It is not a possessive love, but rather a "godmother or helper" (48). Ultimately, she helps the hero through his individuation calling that is outside of the home. In a patriarchal society, these lyrics solidify a women's role in society – one being, to assist with the success of the hero whose life is elevated in society while the women are recessed to the realm of the home.

Idealized Womanhood Caught in the Broken Web

With a more humanized interpretation of the feminine experience, or of the heroine's personal journey, my mother viewed La Virgen de Guadalupe as the chaste and nurturing archetype who would guide her through the individuation stages from maidenhood to motherhood. This virgin goddess served as the bridge from a personal understanding of her experiences as a woman to the greater cultural constructs that defined motherhood. My mother's generation could not speak up about society's double standard that defined a woman's honor, based on whether she was a chaste woman until marriage. For Ramona, La Virgen de Guadalupe was supposed to bring protection, comfort, and hope in the patriarchal world that set double standards for women.

My mother believed herself to be on track of being a virgin when she got married, thus allowing her to wed in the Catholic Church. At twenty years old, she dated her first serious boyfriend. In this relationship, she learned a life-changing experience – that unconsented sex could happen to a woman. Although she had been raised to believe that a woman sacrifices everything for love, she also thought her purity would be protected by La Virgen. She would learn months later that she was pregnant. Unfortunately, the man she had grown to love would not marry her (Martinez). Then the time came for her to act without his consent. She ultimately decided that she would have the child on her own. As a result of her own decision, my mother's life unexpectedly became a contradiction to her societal beliefs. In its place, she had to endure the psychological impacts from the newly acquired stigma. She now had to ward off the judgments of others, including her own family members, as a result of her choice to mother her child on her own. But as the life inside of her grew, so too did her will and determination to become a mother – albeit in an unconventional way.

"*Yo quería casarme de blanco, dentro de una iglesia con la virgencita como mi testigo*" ("I wanted to get married in white, inside of a church with the *Virgencita* as my witness") was how she described the shame and humiliation that dominated her life for decades. This is the consequence for women in a society that honors virginity more than motherhood and teaches women that they must suffer alone. Amid the grave uncertainty of the future, Ramona felt "*sola y abandonada*" ("alone and abandoned"), as she was subject to shame from those she loved (Martinez). When she told me this story, she recalled that no one in her community offered her any guidance, not even the sisters-in-law who were also pregnant at the time. Alone in solitude, she remained too vulnerable and too ashamed to ask for help. No one asked her if she loved him. No one questioned his decision to walk away from her and their child. During that time, it was a well-known fact that men, including her own father, kept a *casa chica*, a little house with a mistress, and often where their illegitimate children lived effectively sequestered from the reality of paternal responsibility. At home, her older brother demanded that she be sentenced to a life of exile, forbidden to live in the family home. In this way, her brother reminded her that her status as a mother with child was disregarded once biology came into the reality. Instead of acknowledging the miracle of a new life, her older brother felt compelled to carry out the narrative written for him by the patriarchy. Fortunately, their mother ignored her son's angry pleas, even as they persisted and grew in aggression. Meanwhile at Ramona's workplace at the women's undergarment warehouse, she was further challenged by coworkers who questioned her marital status when her body began showing the physical signs of pregnancy. They asked, with doubt in their voices, about the husband who no one had ever seen.

With audaciousness, my mother relied on the powers of her imagination. She created socially acceptable narratives and elaborate stories about how she did indeed have a husband who worked out-of-town. She was not deterred by their follow-up questions.

In their writing about the mechanism of shame in *The Female Face of Shame*, Erica L. Johnson and Patricia Moran quote feminist philosopher Sandra Lee Bartkly's description of shame:

> the distressed apprehension of the self as inadequate or diminished: it requires if not an actual audience before whom my deficiencies are paraded, then an internalized audience with the capacity to judge me ... shame requires the recognition that I am, in some important sense, as I am seen to be.
>
> (4)

It is inevitable that we internalize shame. In my mother's case, the internalization of shame meant that despite her ability to imagine a life of a happily-ever-after, the self-punishment and threads of shame were so deeply engrained into the untold parts of her stories, and she remained too powerless to pluck them out.

I am reminded of Maxine Hong Kingston's *The Woman Warrior: Memoirs of a Girlhood among Ghosts*. In the opening chapter, "No Name Woman," Kingston evokes the story of her Chinese aunt. The family denies her existence after she committed the ultimate transgression a woman could commit: to give birth to a child society labels "illegitimate". The night she gave birth, the villagers raided their home:

> The villagers broke in the front and the back doors at the same time, even though we had not locked the doors against them. Their knives dripped with the blood of our animals. They smeared blood on the doors and walls.
>
> (4)

Later "the next morning" she and the baby are found "plugging up the family well" (5). The male side of the family deliberately and systematically erases all traces of her existence. No Name Woman's story would serve as a cautionary tale to women, told by women, to future generations to be reminded of the consequences of bringing shame to the family. Yet, by telling her story, Kingston breaks the silence. She "not only repairs the broken ancestral branch between herself and her 'forerunner,' she breaks the family taboo on naming her aunt and thus defies her family's even more draconian punishment of sentencing the aunt to an eternity of exile" (Johnson and Moran 1).

In contrast to No Name Woman's story, my grandmother, my mother and her child, fought so that mother and child could live. Nonetheless, my mother internalized the way that shameful burdens are imposed on femininity and female embodiment. She kept the shame embedded within herself for decades, as shame would slither into her life, and coil itself around her already protective heart. She would bear the agony of this shame until she would break the silence that was no longer needed, by telling her story. It could be said that No Name Woman would be a metaphorical figure in my mother's psyche, as my mother would sequester and hide away the parts of her that had been shamed. Through breaking her own silence, and finally telling of her own story at 82 years old, she has learned how to absolve the inner and outer destructive forces that are often so inflicted on women by the patriarchal society. In this way, her *testimonio* is the de-shaming narrative that rewrites the plot that had suggested she live a life of dishonor. In telling her own story, my mother has now reached the shores of deeply understanding how shame and self-conviction could have two sides to the same coin. "*Tenerla me hizo sentir como si finalmente tuviera algo que era mío*" ("Having her made me feel like I finally had something that was mine"), is how my mother described feeling about the birth of her beloved daughter (Martinez).

Sacrifices of a Wife and Mother

They first met on Calle Cajeme in Nogales, Sonora, it being the street where they both lived. "*Cuando me conoció por primera vez, tenía mi hija en mis brazos*" ("When he met me for the first time, I had my daughter in my arms"), is the way my mother began the story about how she met my father (Martinez). She was twenty-two, he was nineteen. The two were introduced at a birthday party held in honor of a mutual neighbor. It was their first names that bonded them: Ramon and Ramona. He was tall, slim, with a strong wave in his dark black hair. He wore his signature Levi jeans and a beige-colored cowboy shirt with snap buttons. She, being petite, wore a white A-line dress with black straps. Even though their families lived on the same street, it was their first time crossing paths. When he was ten years old, he had been sent to live with his godmother and godfather on a ranch. It was a common custom at that time for large families to send a child to live with extended family, which resulted in the separation from their mother, father and siblings. In my father's case, his godmother and godfather had no biological children, so my father was sent to live with them. Then, later, he would spend his early adult years using alcohol to numb the charged emotions stemming from the feelings of abandonment caused by this separation. When my parents met, he was gregarious, and her personality was a mixture of being shy and social. But, when in the presence of Mexican *corridos* and *música Norteña*, they both came to life. With the sway of the music, their bodies were able to shed life's sorrows already bestowed upon them, and simply enjoy themselves on the dance floor. He had an elementary school education, and she, albeit due to her peregrinations between cities and countries, had an early junior high school education. They both came from families who prioritized the basic principle of family survival, making an education impossible to achieve. A year later, Ramon and Ramona were married in a small ceremony with a live trio playing in the backdrop. She left behind a household with an alcoholic father, and he left a critical and devouring mother who saw his young wife as an unchaste woman, unworthy of her son's love; a narrative he would later weaponize against her.

When her eldest daughter was old enough to attend school, Ramona had given birth to a second cherished daughter. She now feared her daughters beginning school in Mexico because it meant getting Ramon to move to the United States, away from his mother, would be more difficult, if not impossible. Remaining in Mexico, she intuitively knew it would decrease her daughters' potential for an education that she herself had always yearned for. And above all, it was her greatest desire to move them away from the poverty experienced from her own childhood. Therefore, she did what millions of women were doing in 1965 – she demanded that her daughters get a fair chance for an education, as a path towards a better future and towards freedom.

In the next twenty years, she and my father would have three more daughters and raise them together in Tucson, Arizona. He would provide for their wellbeing as his main priority in life. This meant he would hold up his end of the traditional gender bargain that was written for him. Also true to that gendered standard, he would act in ways that would demean her existence and crush her spirit. She was devoted to her husband, to her children and to God; relative to the image of womanhood that Catholicism accepted. Throughout the twenty-eight years they were married, her first daughter's birth, without a patronym, presented a secret, when revealed, had the power to threaten the entire wellbeing of their family unit. This is because my father, when in a drunken state, used this as intimidation to get my mother to acquiesce to his demands. She was forced to give into his manipulation and threats that he would tell her daughters the truth. Enveloped in fear coupled with an inability to process her own trauma, my mother routinely gave in to him. These violent disagreements were often stormy and a tense environment to my childhood.

Being a seamstress was the creative expressions my mother was allowed to have. So, my mother used this outlet and poured her talent into designing clothes for her daughters. There was no style too difficult or intricate for her; she could design and make jumpsuits with long zippers running along the front side and high-waist tunic dresses. She designed a line of contemporary clothing for her daughters, along with a healthy stock of hand-me-down-dresses. She took such great pride in her designs and dedication to her craft. "*Fue buena pobre*" ("I was a resourceful poor person") is how she described her savviness for saving whatever leftover money from the weekly expenses to make ends meet, and still have money left to purchase the needed materials to make the designs she conjured up (Martinez). The frequent trips to the fabric store were the moments of togetherness spent between her and her daughters. And so, creating and mending our vestments and sewing our clothes was how she expressed her love.

Revelations: Inquiry Into a New Way of Seeing and Being

Throughout the 1980s, for a woman living in an unhappy marriage to find bilingual resources to understand her rights was nonexistent. Instead, she was exposed to possibilities for her freedom through other means. It first began by watching Spanish language talk shows on television where she learned about *el valor de la mujer* ("the value that women possess") (Martinez). Then the most tangible support came when my father began his path towards sobriety. Through the Alcoholics Anonymous meetings that he was attending, my father learned that my mother could participate in Al-Anon, a mutual support program for people whose lives have been affected by someone else's drinking. Through the power of hearing other women's stories in Al-Anon meetings, my mother learned that she had to *"luchar"* (fight) for herself, and in order to better understand her role in his disease. Newly empowered, she knew she, too, must change. This meant that she needed to take a stance against his abuse and threats. She also came to realize that her recovery was tied to his recovery. She remained active in this support group, and even became the treasurer of her local chapter for ten years. However, while he remained sober, the marriage continued to fray. In 1993, they separated for a final time, and a year later, their divorce was final. She paid an attorney with her hard-earned money, and the divorce documents were served and filed.

Following twenty-eight years of marriage, she was alone to recreate the life that had been forbidden to many women of her generation: one of autonomy, away from violence, alcoholism, and the intergenerational trauma of her life. Learning how to build a sense of self and to create a new order in her world would take priority for the next half of her life. Having been raised by an emotionally absent and alcoholic father, she would work toward ridding herself of a lifetime of guilt and shame. She would first have to learn how to become "clean" from the alcoholics that she had been addicted to throughout her life.

She was in her early fifties when her daughters were all living their independent lives. It was also the time of another life changing discovery – a lump on her left breast was found to be cancerous. It had been eight months since her last mammogram. One afternoon, she learned about the importance of self-examination on a Spanish television program. That same afternoon, laying on her bed, she administered a self-examination of her breasts and found a lump. During the next six months, she would rely on her daughters' support. This news came at a time when her sense of self was transforming from sole dependency upon one man, to surrounding herself in a strong community of friends and family. This included my father, who, despite no longer living together, supported her through her surgery and the eight rounds

of chemotherapy treatments that followed. She shared that, during the chemotherapy, the months had three weeks only because the week of chemotherapy was a complete blur as it was spent in recovery from the harsh
side effects, such as severe vomiting, vertigo and fatigue (Martinez). She went
through a mastectomy and reconstruction of her left breast. By summoning
tremendous inner strength through the difficulty and uncertainty of the following months, and years, she prevailed, becoming one of 4 million breast
cancer survivors in the United States (American Cancer Society).

Within six months following her cancer treatments, she began her work in
community activism. Her new work quickly became a part of her creative efforts
toward undoing the harmful narratives about her gender role – one which placed
her only in the home, with no potential for earning her own money, with no sense
of professional womanhood. She worked to give a voice of wisdom and advocacy
on behalf of a Latina women's health group called *Mensajeras de Salud* (Mes-
sengers of Health) for the YWCA. Her role as a community outreach coordi-
nator was to reach out to women in her Spanish speaking community who
needed mammograms; many had reached their fifties without ever having one.
Latina women have the lowest rate of screening than other ethnic groups (Luque
et al.). My mother made and drove women to their appointments. She worked to
build bridges to women's health from their own doorsteps. This gratifying work
went on for over three years until the grant funding ended. Through engaging in
this work, and along the way of self-reflection of her new position in society, she
revealed to me, was the beginning of an awakening to her abilities to gain a
stronger sense of self-worth and financial independence. This marked the beginning of her learning how to break the victim loop and be accountable for herself.
It was a time in her life, which she categorized as the era when "*Aprende a luchar
como mujer*" ("I learned how to fight like a woman") (Martinez).

From the divorce proceedings, my mother kept the family home, the first
home she and my father purchased in 1972. It is a two-bedroom brick home
where they raised all five daughters. Two medium-sized willow trees were
planted in the front yard. In the hot summers, both willows were covered with
cicadas, trying to attract a mate with their high-pitched song. The vibration
was so loud that it drowned out the sounds of the fast-passing cars on 6th
Avenue. The house is located in the south side of Tucson, a predominantly
working-class Latino community and has been subjected to environmental
racism the entire time my parents have owned their home. In the 1990s,
residents claimed they were becoming ill and dying from exposure to tri-
chloroethylene (TCE), an industrial solvent used by industries, whose sites
were commonly situated practically in the backyards of the working-class
communities like my parents.[5] The exposure went on for decades. TCE
exposure is associated with a variety of illnesses and cancers in our community. Because my mother was so busy during that time with raising her
family, coupled with the language barrier, it kept her from seeking information about options for solutions and reparations. My family's story

would never be included in any of the class action lawsuits being filed and settled. Not seeking justice for her family would become a regret she would bear for the rest of her life.[6]

Over the years, she poured her creativity into creating a new home of her own self-expression. She no longer needed to confine herself to the bathroom for privacy; now she had the entire house to herself. Ramona splurged and ordered bottled water. She accessed her creative fire as she stripped the home of its traumatic memories. She repainted the house – one solid color of paint in some rooms and colorful murals in others. She alone would decide who was welcomed inside. She transformed the home into what she now calls "*la casita de mi suños*" ("the house of my dreams") (Martinez). This is particularly true because the house has a tiled mural of the Virgen de Guadalupe, nestled in the red brick façade. During the month of December, she creates an elaborate artistic installation around the figure, including red Christmas lights that outline the edges and with red mini fresh roses interwoven within the string of lights. The other reason she attributes to calling her home "*la casita de mi sueños*" is because that is where she raised her five daughters. On the other hand, her newly found solitude would weigh on her at times, imposing a new meaning of abandonment and fear. However, she learned how to rely on her creativity, and appreciate her space and time, despite the silence.

In the process of creating a new hearth, she learned to access another type of energy, and one that runs deeper. She now embraces some of La Virgen de Guadalupe's other archetypal qualities, such as graciousness, inner mother light, inspiration, and generosity, all stemming from a more secure sense of self. As my mother is emotionally freer now to partake in her own feminine nature, and she feels more at home within, she has bestowed a merciful attitude towards herself. My mother continues to feel loved and cared for by *nuestra madre*, the divine mother energy, calling on her during times of need to share her burdens. Through her devotional practices, she nurtures a witness within herself who knows her own strength. She can turn inward, hold paradoxes, and step into the mysteries of womanhood. Her newfound insights, which she has accessed with her "own heart" echoes the poetics in the following passage by Clarissa Pinkola Estés. Encouraging women to think of "our Nuestra Madre Grande," she writes:

> Think of her not in the ways you've been told/sold.
> Rather, seek her with your own eyes without blinders
> and your own heart without shutters.
> Look low instead of high.
> Look right under your nose.
> She comes in many guises and disguises.
> Hidden, right out in the open.
> *And you will know her immediately by her immaculate*
> *and undivided heart for humanity.*
> (21)

Desahogada: **An Act of Resistance**

"*Desahogada*" (undrowned) is the word my mother used to describe how her body responded to feeling unburdened from the wounds which had left her feeling smothered for decades. This is what she revealed as our interviews for this chapter reached a conclusion. The image of being *desahogada* is of one, alone and without assistance, regaining the capacity to breathe fresh life as an act of resistance after a period of being asphyxiated. It is an image of having the strength to rise above nocturnal waters, like Metis at the pit of Zeus's belly.[7] It is an image of taking in breath, as in a rebirth. Telling her own story was like an awakening towards determining her own orientation, one rooted in dignity and love. Recognizing her own inner light, she could embrace feeling unburdened from a life of shame.

The word "inspiration" comes to mind when I reflect on what it means that she was able to pluck the deep wound from her flesh and soul and feel *desahogada*. Inspiration comes from the Latin word *inspirare*: to inhale or "blow into" (through the lungs), (etymonline). To have space to draw in air is symbolic of having the capacity for the mind and body to breathe in life, spirit, and inspiration, while witnessing the miracles and beauty within one's own life. In this way, the time had come when she, on her own, came to realize not only her power to confront the anger and suffering that kept her identified with her oppressor, my father, but also to let blossom all the unlived life that had been tucked away inside of her.

Throughout the interview process, as she shared her story with me, my mother became more self-aware that tending to her own maternal wound was necessary to setting herself free from the pain she had endured, and had gone unprocessed for generations. She had been raised to contend with the traumatic effects of her parents' unhealed emotional wounds. Then she spent another twenty-eight years whirling in my father's emotional wounds and in his toxic world, trying to make a marriage work against all odds. Post-divorce, for another twenty-five years, she was further weighted down by the aftereffects of having carried anger, resentment and shame all those years. In the telling of her own story, she was able to mark the places where small deaths had occurred. She paused at those moments in her life and mourned what she had tried to forget (the childhood poverty; her father's alcoholism; the crashed car he never apologized for; the years of womanizing; the drunken days; the physical and verbal abuse while he was under the influence of alcohol). In telling her own story, my mother grieved for the intimacy and love not reciprocated from the men she loved in her life. She brought to consciousness her emotional wounds around her mother who worked tirelessly to support her family but who, ultimately, could not protect her. In telling her story, she regained her dignity and ability for self-forgiveness. With this newfound understanding and self-compassion, she was able to move toward the path of forgiving my father, and she could finally stop being a victim. I am reminded of what James Hillman references about the power of stories and the archetypal act that storytelling has to transform our souls:

We are different at the end of the story because the soul has gone through a process during the telling, independent of its syntax and full understanding of its words. Moreover, a narrative account is irreversible: once an event is told into a tale it cannot easily be dislodged from its home, there, always bearing with it echoes of its first telling. Through the telling of events – which is what *mythos* originally meant – the soul takes random images and happenings and makes them into particular lived experiences. The soul needs something more than language games, more than words and speech.

(143)

Through the telling of her own mythos, including the stories of deep regret and of the unprocessed grief inside of her, a profound inner change ensued. She was finally able to call forth the parts of herself that were truncated from her in order to survive, and in this process, a new self-emerged. As she learned to no longer experience shame, loss and longing as the prevailing states of being, her inner world in connection to her body and her sense of self were refigured. Most notably, my mother accessed her memories and embodied her story. She was aware, in Anzaldua's beautiful words, that "for images, words, stories to have this transformative power, they must arise from the human body – flesh and body …" (97). What was once a shame-laden past, was now an invitation for spiritual transformation, connecting her to love all of herself more deeply.

In further contemplation, my mother did not have the language to allow her to communicate shame. I am reminded of Helen Merrell Lynd's work in *On Shame and the Search for Identity* regarding the risks of discovering the ways to communicate shame, and the bearing it has on one's sense of identity. Lynd writes:

[The] lack of a language contributes to the sense of estrangement. If, however, one can sufficiently risk uncovering oneself and sufficiently trust another to seek means of communicating shame, the risking of exposure can be in itself an experience of release, expansion, self-revelation, a coming forward of belief in oneself, and entering into the mind and feeling of another person.

(249)

On her journey to reaching the other side of shame and suffering, my mother took on the risk to pin things to the earth. In doing so, she learned how to trust her psyche to confront life's traumas. In her newly found *fuerza* ("strength"), she could move more deeply into her sense of self and find the words to make conscious truths that were previously unconscious. Through telling her story, and by trusting the storytelling process, and me, her psyche was relieved of this burden that she no longer needed to carry. She could allow herself to now know, in full consciousness, what she knew. In the process of telling her story, she began to trust in her ability to overcome shame and trauma, and in its place, heal her inner wounds.

Throughout the years, the unprocessed grief and trauma had blocked not only her ability for having intimacy with parts of herself, but also with her daughters. All those years, we bore her open reproaches against our father. Throughout the years, she had quietly relied on her daughters for her own emotional support by oversharing with us, bringing about what some psychologists call "emotional incest" (Buqué 129). This is "when children take on the role of an intimate partner with whom the parent can share all their worries and insecurities" (Buqué 129). Her oversharing of her resentment and anger towards our father led to creating an unabridged distance between us, even when our father was diagnosed with prostate cancer. When my sisters and I summoned our support for him, she treated us like traitors to her enemy who needed to be punished. She, in turn, treated us with resentment, a hurtful coldness, which felt like love was being held back, and with an exchange of perpetual disparaging remarks about him and the pain he had caused her. Telling her life story has allowed her to finally feel unburdened. She now has a clearer path to seek greater authenticity with her daughters. Beginning anew, she makes efforts to offer me emotional support, her own resilience, and words from a heart that has begun to grieve its own sorrows.

In a new "*desahogada*" state, she now has the clarity of her deepest desire – one of having stronger and more genuine relationships with her adult daughters. Knowing that she had emotionally strayed away from them for far too long, she hopes to see them through the emotional closeness that she now holds within herself. Because she can begin to love the different parts within herself, she is able to endeavor the process to move closer to the facets of her daughters that she had previously been unable to acknowledge. Today she recognizes that she is freer to accept her daughters' love and reciprocate back from a newly discovered place of self-love, rather than from the previous stifled state of shame and loneliness.

Bearing Witness to Generational Change

For a vast part of her life, my mother had suffered the distress of having to keep her story tucked away only in the crevices of her own heart. As captured in the epigraph of this chapter, Zora Neale Hurston proposed that "there is no greater agony than bearing an untold story inside of you" (176). Our stories, Hurston seemed to know, are a way to know ourselves and each other. My mother had borne the pain stemming from a profound sense of isolation. In telling her story, she not only registered her grief and trauma, but she was able to set free the burdens that kept her anchored in suffering, leaving her unable to travel towards a new life.

By re-mapping some of the pivotal individuation experiences she shared with me, she regained a dignity that was hers all along. She fulfilled a desire within that she had quietly clung to for decades: the ability to tell her own story, one filled with misrepresented patriarchal distortions of womanhood. She also acknowledged that the life she has lived as an ordinary human being is valuable and worthy of being shared.

At the conclusion of our final interview, my mother expressed relief from the agony she bore from carrying her untold story:

> *Llevo años queriendo contar mi historia, pero no sabía cómo hasta que te interesastes en mi vida. Me sentia asfixiada, como si me hubiera estado ahogando todos estos años. Durante años pensé: "¿Moriré sin contar mi historia?" Finalmente, me siento desahogada.*
>
> (I have been wanting to tell my story for years, but I didn't know how until you became interested in my life. I felt like I had been suffocating, drowning all these years. For years, I wondered if I would die without telling my story. Finally, I feel like my head is above water.)

(Martinez)

Notes

1 From *Dust Tracks on a Road* by Zora Neale Hurston. Copyright (c) 1942 by Zora Neale Hurston; renewed (c) 1970 by John C. Hurston. Used by permission of HarperCollins Publishers.
2 In 1922 the Yucatan was the first state to give women "limited" voting rights (Pablos 97).
3 In many accounts the "precious Spanish flower" is a rose.
4 This is the coarse fabric that Juan Diego wore on which the Virgen's image miraculously appeared.
5 The chemicals TCE, 1,4-dioxane and per- and polyfluorinated alkyl substances (PFAS) – harmful chemicals used in nearby industrial and defense-related processes – were spilled or leaked onto the ground since the early 1950s, making their way into area groundwater. The community of Tucson relies on groundwater as its primary source of water for domestic, industrial and irrigation use. These chemicals were discovered in 1983 in water wells in the area near my parents' home at levels above what is considered safe by the EPA for drinking water quality under the Safe Drinking Water Act (EPA). Testing for PFAS did not begin until 2019 (ADEQ). Wells were shut down or taken out of service by the City of Tucson in the mid-1980s (EPA), after at least 30 years of potential exposure to the community.
6 This has impacted both of my parents, who have each had their battles with cancer. As for the rest of our family, we all have experienced autoimmune illnesses that are tied to the toxic drinking water we consumed while living in this community.
7 I look closely at the myth of Zeus swallowing Metis in Chapter 4.

References

ADEQ. "Superfund Site: Tucson International Airport Area." 2024. Retrieved from https://azdeq.gov/superfund/TIAA.

American Cancer Society. "Key Statistics for Breast Cancer." 2024. Retrieved from www.cancer.org/cancer/types/breast-cancer/about/how-common-is-breast-cancer.html#xd_co_f=Y2Q1OWM4Y2UtYmRjNi00YTRjLWE3N2UtYzk1ODE1OThkODc3~.

Anzaldúa, Gloria. *Borderlands/La Frontera: The New Mestiza.* San Francisco. Aunt Lute Books. 1999.

Buqué, Mariel. *Break the Cycle: A Guide to Healing Intergenerational Trauma.* New York. Dutton. 2024.

Castillo, Ana. *Goddess of the Americas: La Diosa de las Américas.* New York. Riverhead Books. 1996.

EPA. "Superfund Site: Tucson International Airport Area." 2024. Retrieved from http s://cumulis.epa.gov/supercpad/cursites/csitinfo.cfm?id=0900684.

Estés, Clarissa Pinkola. *Untie the Strong Woman: Blessed Mother's Immaculate Love for the Wild Soul.* Boulder. Sounds True. 2011.

Herrera-Sobek, María. *The Mexican Corrido: A Feminist Analysis.* Indianapolis. Indiana University Press. 1990.

Hillman, James. *Re-visioning Psychology.* New York. Harper & Row. 1975.

Hurston, Zora Neale. *Dust Tracks on a Road: A Memoir.* New York. Amistad. 2006.

Inspirare. Inspiration. Retrieved from www.etymonline.com/search?q=inspiration. Accessed April 2023.

Johnson, Erica L. and Patricia Moran. *The Female Face of Shame.* Indianapolis. Indiana University Press. 2013.

Kingston, Maxine Hong. *The Woman Warrior: Memoirs of a Girlhood among Ghosts.* New York. Vintage Press. 1989.

Luque, John S., Ayaba Logan, Grace Soulen, Kent E. Armeson, Danielle M. Garrett, Caroline B. Davila and Marvalla E. Ford. "Systematic Review of Mammography Screening Educational Interventions for Hispanic Women in the United States." *Journal of Cancer Education* 34(3) (2019): 412–422.

Lynd, Helen Merrell. *On Shame and the Search for Identity.* New York. Harcourt. 1958.

Martinez, Ramona. Personal interview. Spring 2022.

Mistral, Gabriela. *Woman.* New York. White Pine Press. 2000.

Pablos, Julia Tuñón. *Women in Mexico: A Past Unveiled.* Austin. University of Texas Press. 1987.

Poole, Stafford. *Our Lady of Guadalupe: The Origins and Sources of a Mexican National Symbol, 1531–1797.* Tucson. University of Arizona Press. 1996.

Rodriguez, Jeanette. "Guadalupe: The Feminine Face of God." *Goddess of the Americas: La Diosa de las Américas.* Ed. Ana Castillo. New York. Riverhead Books. 1996.

Chapter 4

In Search of My Mother's Mythos

(Tucson, Arizona and Santa Barbara, California)

Tan chiquita y tan valiente.

(An expression told to me by my mother)

While my mother did not come of age reading Simone de Beauvoir's *The Second Sex*, her life has been heading for the same vague destination: towards freedom. Growing up in Mexico with life-defining poverty, my mother's social standing meant her life was predisposed to the gendered cultural imperatives of domesticity and motherhood. In my familial constellation, my mother was physically present, but emotionally distant. Yet she was devoted to her daughters and to her husband. My father was the breadwinner of our household. He was hardworking, never short of work. My mother's attitude toward my father was that he was a force to be reckoned with in silence, as his points of view were to remain unchallenged. He was adequately comfortable with his masculine side; my mother, the embodiment of the feminine virtues of her time.

Growing up, witnessing my father devalue my mother left me feeling like the feminine signpost in my early life was obscured. That is, it was difficult to embrace a strong sense of feminine knowing, as it is transmitted by a pivotal figure like a mother. Our household had a domineering father who benefited, like all patriarchal systems, by keeping my mother in a place of subordinance. However, a desire to align with my own matrilineal legacy has led me to seek a deeper understanding of my mother, as the woman with whom I share my creation myth. Specifically, I wanted to reclaim the emotional landscape that my mother and I share. Through this process, I hoped to acquaint myself with my mother's identity as a woman, separate from her identity as my mother. Along this path of discovering who she is, besides being my mother, I have sought to recognize my own layered womanhood. I have also sought insights into the ways that internalizing family politics shapes our lives. In essence, my search for my matrilineal legacy has landed me into the center of a deep part of myself. To appreciate my own trajectory of the search for a matrilineal line, I have started by remembering my personal mother, her mythos (the stories and beliefs that make up her sense of herself), and my emotional and psychological proximity to her.

DOI: 10.4324/9781003255857-4

A Maternal Wound Shaped by *Vergüenza* (Shame) and Betrayal

While raising me, my mother hid her wounds and her vulnerabilities, leaving much of herself unknowable, unreachable. Her way of teaching me the patriarchal rules for women was to instill Catholic values of virtue that she herself had been taught and tried to live by all her life. To my mother, I was to live life entangled in the same broken web of the patriarchal culture that aims to subvert women's opportunities to live freely. She taught me that men are to be served. She trained me to believe that my body was to remain hidden, unknown, and unspoken about. As an adolescent, my menstruating body went unaccounted for, a mystery to be grappled with on my own. When her response as to what I was to do with my developing and changing teenage body was met under a cloud of silence, shame bubbled up inside of me. By the time I reached high school, her censorious behavior towards all things related to my body had conveyed shame in me.

Of course, my mother had many things to contend with: a demanding husband; five daughters with unique needs and anxieties; and her own inner struggles. My mother's dark, worried brown eyes were the barometer of the family's emotional life. In the kitchen, she often cooked in silence, drowning out the cacophony of the household with the sonorous voice of Vicente Fernandez playing on a cassette tape in the background. At times, she commanded my obedience by exuding a coldness that felt like a withholding of love. Other times, as she spoke to me, her face would cast a disapproving gaze, with curt and cold sentences. In those moments, I often registered emotional shame in the maternal mirror. In *The Emotionally Absent Mother*, Jasmine Lee Cori writes that mirroring and self-validating relationships between mothers and daughters is the basis for our self-esteem and self-acceptance (11). Feeling seen by our mothers helps us recognize a basic level of our existence. When my mother went silent, I felt abandoned. Later, as an adult, and as I began contending with my maternal wound, I began to better understand those were the moments when my mother needed to turn inward, as she was reaching for inner strength and coping strategies.

In *Shame: The Power of Caring*, Gershen Kaufman explains that "identification begins within the family. Learning how to become a person originates through identification, as we first identify, and, thereby, have a beginning base from which to navigate the human world" (38). He posits that one source of shame is "from parental rejection of the child's most fundamental needs, however unconscious that rejection may be" (142). While both of my parents communicated shame and shaped my "parental climate," in Kaufman's terms, this chapter focuses on exploring the distorted mirroring I received from my mother (38). My maternal wound, and, in particular, my relationship with my mother have been the impetus of an inability – that lasted decades – to look away from the shortcomings I saw in both her and me. There was a central tension between my mother and me that stemmed from my desire for her to stand up for herself.

What is more, I had internalized my mother's own shame. In doing so, I began to realize that gaining my independence and my grasp on womanhood meant that I would have to speak up and act against the patriarchal views of women. In *Borderlands: La Frontera*, Gloria Anzaldúa writes, "[d]ominant paradigms, predefined concepts that exist as unquestionable, unchallengeable, are transmitted to us through the culture. Culture is made by those in power" (38). And while men create the cultural rules by which we live, it is often mothers that pass down the disempowering beliefs about ourselves. Our mothers perpetuate cultural rules and messages when we hear them "tell their sons to beat their wives for not obeying them, for being *hociconas* (big mouths), for being *callejeras* (going to visit and gossip with neighbors), for expecting their husbands to help with the rearing of children and the house-work, for wanting to be something other than housewives" (38). These were the cultural expectations of my mother's generation that I was exposed to growing up. And these were also the experiences, like tributaries, that fed into the confluence that shaped my maternal wound. Yet, despite knowing now that my mother was fated to imprint these cultural messages onto me, I still felt that she had betrayed me for teaching me these feelings of shame for being a woman.

One way to better understand – metaphorically – the theme of women and betrayal in Mexican culture lies in the story of La Malinche. La Malinche, or Doña Marina after her Christian baptism, became the translator for Hernán Cortés. She could speak a Mayan language and Nahuatl and was "absorbing Spanish," writes Grisel Gómez-Cano in *The Return to Coatlicue: Goddesses and Warladies in Mexican Folklore* (135). La Malinche, Gómez-Cano writes, "was given as a slave to Cortés when she was an adolescent, perhaps nineteen years old" (135). She "became something like, but more than, the secretary of state, shrewdly counseling him on diplomacy with the Indians ..." (135). By proving her loyalty and respect for him, the story says, she is "responsible for the downfall of the Mexican Empire, and thus she is associated with lust, evil, and death" (211). La Malinche has kept an enduring hold as a motif in our imagination for betrayal, sexual exploitation, and survival. In *Native Country of the Heart*, Cherríe Moraga poignantly writes that Malinche:

> wrestles inside the collective unconscious of every Mexican female. She murmurs in a distant indiscernible voice that the official story is not the whole story; that Malinche was not free and was proffered freedom for her services. We hear the devil's temptation in the tale; that our sex is our sin and our salvation ...
>
> (16)

Moraga importantly reminds us that Malinche is given away by her father. She writes: "In this story, the Mexican man uses his daughter to do the step-ping and the fetching. He sells her out to do his bidding. And he remains uncompromised" (16–17). How Malinche later learns to survive the betrayal of having been given up by her father is to "talk out of both sides of her mouth. *They made me a slave and condemn me when I act like one*" (17). This is also how our mothers learned to survive. Moraga reflects: "*I come from a long line of vendidas.* I inscribe these words as an act of Chicana feminist reclamation, naming the women in my *familia* as traitors within an impossible patriarchy" (20). I contend that what mothers also learned within the "impossible patriarchy," is to communicate with their daughters through a similar mode of double talk and through actions with multiple meanings. Therefore, if we want to understand our mothers, and the context from which they raised us, we must learn to decipher the language from which they learned to speak.

When I was in my twenties and thirties, living alone in California, I traveled to Europe and South America alone. My mother's typical response to my life was that I was always *sola* (alone). In her next breath, however, she would utter words of admiration, even while speaking in her most judgmental tone: "*tan chiquita y tan valiante*" (so small and so valiant). She recognized my independence, but yet, at the same time, was critical that I did not have a partner. I wondered if she saw the parts of me that were learning how to be *sola* (alone) with myself. My life was not attached to the appearances of safety, "protection" by a man or through the structures of motherhood, the essential foundations my mother had built her life around. I was seeking the life of an artist, searching for my voice, inspiration and adventure. When she added *tan chiquita y tan valiante*, she inscribed a blended message. On the one hand, this told me that my mother could see me as strong, brave, and independent (how I was yearning to be seen in the world). Yet, on the other, her description of me as "chiquita" (small*ness*), resonated. My 5 foot 4 inch stature was symbolic of how I was made to feel as a Mexican-American woman living in the United States. What I had learned from my mother in those early years was how to hide my dreams, fears, and insecurities. I had learned to identify with the sense of powerlessness. At the time, it was challenging to identify with any part of my mother's life as creatively empowering to me. I feared that the life of the female artist pays a price, and that during those years, she would not support me.[1]

Throughout the interview process, and while listening to my mother's *testimonio*, to write the chapter for this book (Chapter 3), I approached her with a deep curiosity to learn about her as a woman, not merely as my mother.[2] In discovering and re-covering her story about womanhood, including her hopes, dreams, and disillusionment of love, I realized a story about a woman with multifarious experiences and desires. I encountered the stories about how she had learned to love herself in an imperfect world. I unearthed a more complete portrait of a woman who had learned to be independent, and to find strength in herself. I was also able to better recognize what she had done for our family and most recently, for herself. I learned more about a pivotal decision that she made for our family; in 1965, my mother spearheaded our immigration from Mexico to the United States so her daughters could get an education. In an era when second-wave feminists were rediscovering Virginia Woolf and Sor Juana Inez de la Cruz, and BIPOC (Black, Indigenous and people of color) feminists were demanding that their identities be represented by their education, my mother was fighting for an education not for herself, but for her daughters. Interestingly, I grew up believing it was my father who initiated and orchestrated this difficult and heroic transition. Instead, it was she who made the risk-taking actions for her family. It was she who possessed the green card required for our family to emigrate from Mexico to the United States. It was she who secured housing for our family and a job for my father. And, it was she who claimed herself, by responding to the oppression and poverty before she even knew how to speak of it. It was an individuation move that she took, before ever having answers to the paradoxes of her – and her daughters' – lives. I now understand that the double talk within our family histories and narratives means that, at times, fathers are taught, consciously or unconsciously, to usurp our mothers' strengths. In other cases, they hide our mothers' strengths so that we cannot identify with them. Since my mother had not been taught how to protect herself from patriarchal distortions of womanhood, she could not openly guide me in a new direction. She could, however, take actions, at the time, and hope that one day I would unearth and decode such double meanings. When I rearranged my family's immigration story, placing my mother as the central protagonist, a counternarrative was revealed: it disclosed the costs of patriarchy upon the feminine psyche within my family. While reckoning with what I had perceived as deficiencies in her, I also saw her strengths. Yet, before discovering parts of my mother which remained hidden, I spent decades feeling betrayed by her earlier disloyalty to me. I acted out as a resentful daughter because I was fearful that I would also betray myself.

The Resentful Daughter

My mother was 31 years old when she gave birth to me. In my earliest emotional memories, I am swimming in a sea of fear, riding waves of grief for having been abandoned by my mother, who is there, but not there. In my young adult years, I was keenly aware of my feelings of low self-worth. The explanation I gave myself was that my mother had not transmitted a strong sense of self-esteem to me. I resented that she seemed self-absorbed, powerless, and unavailable to support me throughout my own challenging times. I dwelt in her shortcomings. I witnessed sorrowful eyes that carried pain, anger, and fear. I struggled between feeling great empathy for her and a yearning for my own teenage self to be seen and supported. Feelings of not being enveloped in maternal support and nourishment categorized my life through adulthood. I had the same disorienting feelings that Nathalie Léger writes about when she describes her feelings towards her mother in *The White Dress*:

> I don't remember anything imposing or sacred, any virtue ... I didn't always love my mother. She was on the side of the losers ... I couldn't bring myself to hug her or console her, she seemed to have shrunk from the shame of having been left ...
>
> (88)

In my resentful stage, I was haunted by images of my mother's emotional pain, which, at the time, stemmed first from my father's inability to love and respect her. Then she was filled with anger towards him after their marriage dissolved (they divorced when I was in my mid-twenties). She frowned at the mention of him as she blamed him for all her losses: of love, of her family, and of her dreams. While she drowned in loneliness and shame, I felt invisible.

Although it was not my mother's fault that her pain and shame were the reasons we seemed to betray each other, her suffering led me to question my own ability to escape a life overwhelmed by the same grievances. I am reminded of Sofia in *Hot Milk* by Deborah Levy, and her fear of absorbing her mother's pain and inheriting her grief. She inevitably resents her mother, Rose. Sofia wonders, in a tone of exasperation:

> Grievance. Grief. Grieving. She more or less inhabited a building called Grievance Heights. Is this where I will have to live, too? Is it? Has Rose already put my name down for an apartment in Grievance Heights? What if I can't afford to live anywhere else? I must remove my name from that waiting list, that long queue of forlorn daughters trailing back to the beginning of time.
>
> (Levy 126)

In her hopelessness, Sofia fears she will not be "bold enough to make a bid for the things [she] wanted to happen" in her own life (128). For a long time, I too lingered in the "queue of forlorn daughters" (126). From my maternal wound, I blamed my mother with the crime of coldness, and accusations of weakness, subverting a desire to sense myself as capable of creating my own life, one autonomous from her pain, shame, and grief.

My father's disrespectful, and oftentimes abusive, behavior towards my mother heightened my fear of sharing in her fate as a woman and a wife. In *Beyond the Myths: Mother–Daughter Relationships in Psychology, History, Literature and Everyday Life*, Shelley Phillips writes that fathers play an "influential role in their daughter's self-esteem through their attitudes to their wives as mothers, as women and as sexual beings" (88). In this sense, as Phillips claims, "if fathers respect their wives and honor them to their daughters, the mother-daughter relationship is stronger" (92). As a child, I was aware of my father's overall *machismo*, his domineering and toxic masculine pride that was strapped over my mother's and my life. For example, I knew that the reason she did not have financial autonomy was due to his forbiddance of her working outside our home. I also knew that when we did not have access to the car during the day while he was at work, it was because he had purposely taken the keys with him, most likely in retaliation and punishment for something he interpreted as a deviation in her behavior. Phillips notes that "the underlying negative messages about mothers lead some daughters to a devalued sense of their femaleness" (90). This was certainly true for me. Watching my mother abdicate respect made me believe she warranted this mistrust. And while I could not consider whether his frustration and anger towards her was justified by her passiveness, I did begin to internalize his behavior towards her as also directed towards me and my gender.

During my teenage years, I blamed my father for my mother's lack of self-esteem, and I did not want my life to assume any likeness to hers. Perhaps it was because I felt the feminine being rejected in my home that made me want to align with my father's charisma and position of power. This was the start of my negative mother complex. At the time, my mother's life echoed that of the protagonist in *The Broken Web*, by Helena Maria Viramontes. This poignant story captures the ways that the lives of Mexican women are tied to structures of power and oppression, entangled in the broken web of religion, culture, and patriarchy. Responding to her husband's abuse, the narrator vacantly reflects: "How could she explain to him that she was so tired and wrinkled and torn by him, his God, his words?" (60). My mother, after having been dispirited by my father, also found that words alone could not capture the weight of his power on her soul. And like in *The Broken Web*, my mother, like the protagonists, "could not leave him because she no longer owned herself" (60). My father had failed to live up to her expectations. And while my mother could not utter her disappointment in words, the weight of the deep and long sighs that punctuated her silence did.

Yet, despite all my father's shortcomings, while growing up in South Tucson, it was my father to whom I felt closer. At a young age, I spent a lot of time with him. As a predominantly Spanish speaker and an entrepreneur, he relied on me to interpret for him on most (if not all) of his business affairs.[3] It did not matter to him that a thirteen-year-old girl did not know the least bit about negotiating with his clients in English, who in those days were mostly white clients from the north side of town who lived in houses at least three times the size of ours. During those years, we moved around in his world, with my voice relaying his messages between the two languages. Then when he needed me to translate and write out his contracts, it also did not matter to him that I had no experience in legal contract writing. He had me write his estimates for the jobs that he bid on. During the first few years, I wrote them by hand. Then he decided that his quotes needed to look more professional. He willingly bought a typewriter, and I taught myself how to type. In those early years, unbeknownst to me, my father was training me to be his permanent employee. This would have left me unable to conjure dreams of my own, for a life of my own. But I escaped from under his vision one week after my twentieth birthday when I initiated the separation from my parents. I fled Tucson for California, where I have lived ever since. To better understand my complicated bond with the staunch patriarch and its hold on my family and my imagination, I turn to the Greek Goddess, Athena, who is born out of her father's head because he had swallowed her mother, Metis.

Athena, Born from Her Father's Head: The Retrieval of Metis, Athena's Mother

Myths express archetypal material, informing an understanding of patterns in the psyche. "They give an account of the archetypal story in the case history, the myth in the mess," writes James Hillman in *Re-visioning Psychology* (101). It follows then, that we approach myths to find new meaning to our experiences. By rethinking and positioning archetypes alongside personal experiences, we engage the myth-making process in our lives. The mythmaker reframes personal stories that are expressed through archetypes, revealing how our lives align with mythic patterns. Hillman points out that "the soul needs something more than language games, more than words and speech. Psychological living implies living in a fantasy, a story, being told by a myth" (143). Also, we know that myths have the strength to move us away from literal objectivity, where we can touch deeper truths. Myths, Hillman writes, are where "[r]ather than an increase of certainty, there is a spread of mystery, which is both the precondition and the consequence of revelation" (142). Of course, aligning our experiences with the archetypal does not mean we lose the specificity or the uniqueness of our subjective experiences.[4] Essentially, since we turn to myths to seek knowledge of our archetypal experiences, I, therefore, invite Athena's myth to help orient the story of my personal genesis.

The most canonized version of the myth, and the one memorialized in the statuary of the Parthenon, is that Athena has a male mother. As it goes, "Her Life as the lightning was flashed from the light of her Father's head" (Harrison 302). Athena's birth from Zeus's head is a mythological representation of a daughter coming into this world exclusively via a patrilineage, and, as a result, she heavily identifies with her father. In this version of the myth, Athena is associated with favoring her father's masculine ways. She is aligned with logic and order. She is celebrated as the goddess of reason, light, and liberty (Harrison 302). A close look at her myth, however, reveals a deeper understanding of women grappling with an over-identification with the masculine aspect of a patriarchal-ordered world. I look at Athena also because reflecting on her myth is a reminder that we too must understand the relationship between our own creativity (as a feminine quality) and the power structures that distort our understanding of ourselves. We know that there are varying versions of myths; this version, the one that says Athena is born of Zeus's head, strips her of a matriarchal lineage. So where is her mother? To that, I will return, but first, it is important to understand Athena's origins a little closer.

In Classic Greek art, there are two distinct images of Athena. One of them is the "helmeted and girdled goddess, with firm stride and massive shield, the unvanquished virgin warrior as guardian of the city ..." (Baring and Cashford 332). The "older image," according to Baring and Cashford in *The Myth of the Goddess: Evolution of an Image,* is of "a wild and awesome goddess, wreathed in snakes, where snakes wind around her head as hair and crown ..." (332). While Athena is known to have been a "direct descendant of the Minoan snake goddess," the Classical tale of her birth takes on another dimension (334–335). These serpentine features prompt questions such as: Who was this earlier Athena (not the one from the popular telling of the myth), and how (and why) was she subject to such profound transformation? Evoking Athena's early expression helps us understand the Athena that represents the need to remember her relationship with her mother.

In *Prolegomena to the Study of Greek Religion*, Jane Harrison tells Athena's origin story this way:

> To tell the story of the making of Athene is to trace the history of the city of Athens ... its political rather than its religious development. At first the maiden of the elder stratum, she has to contend for supremacy with a god of that stratum, Poseidon, who was the god of the ancient aristocracy of Athens, an aristocracy based, as they claimed descent from Poseidon, on patriarchal condition.
>
> (301)

This flourishing democracy of Athens revived the ancient figure of Kore, which is Athene's other name, Pallas, the Kore, or maiden, of the clan of the Pallantidea, the foes of Athenian Theseus (Harrison 301). In this revival of Athena from an ancient figure of the Kore, Harrison writes, "they [the Greeks] made her a sexless thing, neither man nor woman; she is laden with attributes like the Parthenos of Pheidias, charged with intended significance, but to the end she remains manufactured, unreal and never convinces us" (Harrison 302). Furthermore, Harrison questions how much we can trust Athena herself for being linked to solely the patrilineal. She writes: "[w]e cannot love a goddess who on principle forgets the Earth from which she sprang; always her lips of the Lost Leader we hear the shameful denial":

> There is no mother bore me for her child,
> I praise the Man in all things (save for marriage),
> Whole-hearted am I, strongly for the Father.
>
> (303)

Here, Athena denies having a mother. In this more familiar version of the myth, the Mother is stripped of her birth-giving powers. We know from being born from her father, that Athena has "praised the Man in all things (save for marriage)" who is given credit for her strength, providing the explanation for her allegiance to her father. She is, as Marion Woodman stated in an interview, "a father's daughter. Her home is in her intellect" (Sieff 182).

Ironically, Athena does indeed have a mother; however, it is a lesser-known detail in her origin myth. In her work *The Goddess: Mythological Images of the Feminine*, Christine Downing references the process of diving deeper into Athena's origin myth as a metaphor of a soulful experience. She writes:

> Athena, in a sense, represents this: the repression of the feminine and the undoing of the repression as a soul task … To recover the Athena who is mothered by Metis and not only fathered by Zeus is to recover ourselves.
> (110)

Athena's matrilineal line, including her relationship to her own femininity, "are mostly hidden and need to be uncovered by careful research and interpretation," Downing aptly notes (110). This lesser-known story about Metis, her mother, makes her representative of what I have been suggesting throughout this work: the search for the absent stories, our mother's mythos, which make up such an important part of our feminine identity, becomes a move towards individuation.

To get a deeper understanding of Metis, Athena's mother, I look to her myth as told by Hesiod, the great poet of the eighth century BCE, in *Theogony* (Baring and Cashford 335). In his poem, he recounts that Metis is the daughter of Oceanus and Teths, that Metis is Zeus's first wife, and that Zeus "thrust her down/into his belly":

> Now Zeus, king of the gods, first took to wife
> Metis, wisest of all, of gods and men.
> But when she was about to bear her child
> Grey-eyed Athena, he deceived her mind
> With clever words and guile, and thrust her down
> Into his belly, as he was advised
> By earth and starry Heaven. In that way
> They said, no other god than Zeus would get
> The Royal power over all the gods
> Who live for ever. For her fate would be
> To bear outstanding children, greatly wise.
> First a girl, Tritogeneia, the grey-eyed,
> Equal in spirit and intelligence
> To Zeus her father …
> But Zeus, forestalling danger, put her down

Into his belly, so that the goddess could
Counsel him in both good and evil plans ...
But Zeus himself produced, from his own head,
Grey-eyed Athene, fearsome queen who brings
The noise of war and, tireless, leads the host,
She who loves shouts and battling and fighting.

                                        (Baring and Cashford 335)

In Greek mythology, Metis is known as the Goddess that embodies cunning intelligence, known as *mêtis*, the word for wisdom and cunning (Dolmage 9).[5] In the popular myth, it is stated that Zeus marries Metis because it is her cunning that will help him and the other Olympic Gods be victorious over the Titans.[6] Metis tricks Cronos, who came to power by castrating his own father, Uranus. To escape the same fate that is, having his son usurp his power, Cronos swallows all of his children, including Zeus.[7] Metis tricks Cronos to "disgorge" the "children whom he had swallowed, and with the aid of his siblings, Zeus waged the war against Cronus and the other Titans" (Apollodorus 9). Furthermore, following this 10-year war, "Zeus was allotted the dominion of the sky ..." (Apollodorus 11). When he marries Metis, Zeus is aware of her power and strength. As noted by Jay Dolmage in "Metis, Mêtis, Mestiza, Medusa: Rhetorical Bodies Across Rhetorical Traditions," Zeus respected and feared Metis because of her pivotal role in defeating the Titans. He also "foresaw the threat her children would be to him, having inherited her mêtis," (wisdom and cunning) (9). When Metis is pregnant with Athena, Zeus is aware that his first-born child could seize him.

Because Zeus feared Metis's power, just as his father before him, he swallowed her to preserve the patriarchy. He swallows Metis, "wisest of all ... into his belly, so that the goddess could/Counsel him in both good and evil plans" (Baring and Cashford 335). However, because of her wisdom, which he desires for himself, he decides she can live as a woman's voice, inside of a man's head, while her body remains hidden. This myth, like all myths, has relevance. It illuminates a legacy of attitudes and psychological implications and assumptions in our lives. Metis, having been swallowed and living inside of Zeus's body, echoes the image my mother describes in Chapter 3 of feeling as if she were swallowed and drowning her entire life (*"senti que me estaba ahogando"*). It is an image of the feminine battling for survival in an environment where her own power is co-opted and appropriated by the patriarchal power. It is crucial to note that the details in Hesiod's poem that reference Metis, Athena's mother, are notably absent from Homer's telling of the myth. Instead, Homer calls Athena "'the daughter of the powerful father'" (Baring and Cashford 336). Yet, in Hesiod's telling of the myth, we are provided with a point of view that German philosopher of history Johann Bachofen calls the established order of "Father-right" over the "Mother-right" (Baring and Cashford 336). Also, one cannot help but see the similarities between Zeus swallowing the pregnant mother and birthing his own daughter, and the birth of Eve from Adam's rib. In both myths, as noted by Baring and Cashford, Athena and Eve are each associated with the serpent: "sometimes the serpent could even stand instead of Athena, and in Genesis, the serpent often has the face of Eve, though the meaning given to the two images in the two traditions is very different" (335). Both myths strip "Mother" Nature from her birth-giving power, which is instead usurped by the male.

Athena, like many women, has been caught in the myth of having been derived from her father alone. In my life, this had manifested into an over-identification with my father's ways of being. I viewed his dedication and efforts towards his work, outside of the house, as having more value than the work my mother was committed to do, inside of our house. And like my father, I was also quick to disparage my mother. While growing up, I was quick to interpret many of her actions as gestures of weakness, and his commanding presence as strength. Recovering Athena's matrilineal history is a symbolic path towards gaining a fuller sense of her and, by extension, of ourselves. We know that Athena has inherited the expressions of her own masculine qualities, such as physical strength, self-confidence, and logic from her father. *In Gyn/Ecology: The Metaethics of Radical Feminism*, Mary Daly writes that by being "male-identified, employing priests, not priestesses, urging men on in battle, siding against women consistently," Athena becomes "Zeus's obedient mouthpiece" (13). The pivotal question becomes: what does Athena gain by knowing the virtues of her matrilineal legacy? Metis is clever, wise counsel, and associated with water through her own mother Tethys, Goddess of fresh water. Metis gives Athena access to a wellspring of feminine intuition, creativity and wisdom as she is "attuned to subtleties and transformations, sensitive to nuances of per-sonal feeling, poetic rather than abstract, receptive rather than commanding" (Downing 117). These are feminine qualities from which Athena is cut off in a world that is oriented towards overvaluing the masculine.

Interestingly, Athena's association (and disassociation) with her mother not only reminds us that she has a mother to claim in her lineage, but also that she herself is not a mother. I appreciate Christine Downing's interpretation of this aspect of Athena's existence to shed light on her as a goddess not of "procrea-tion, but of creation" (118). While Athena has been seen as a local fertility goddess, Downing notes that "by the time Athena is Athena, she represents a different kind of creativity" (118). She is rather "Athena Ergane, the worker, the maker, and, as such, connected to soul, to soul-work" (118). What is of great concern to Athena is the "outwarding of soul, its expression and realiza-tion in what we do and make" (118). She is also the prototype of the artistically creative woman, which invites a deeper understanding of my ambivalence towards my tendency to mistrust the feminine within and a tendency to over identify with the masculine aspects of myself. I see Athena as one of the god-desses who can teach us about what it means to align with a lost matrilineal lineage to propel the soul's creative work towards claiming our full potential.

The focus on Athena's myth, as if she was solely born by her father, represents one of the Western myths where women are depotentiated as creators. Mary Daly calls this type of erasure of women-as-creators, a form of "mind-binding." She likens this destruction to the foot binding, which "mutilated millions of Chinese women for a thousand years" for the pleasure of men (Daly 8).[8] Uncovering our mother's stories, (undoing of the "mind binding") sets into motion an ability to re-member our own relationship to our personal mothers, take pride in them, and by extension, to the feminine as a way of being within ourselves. Importantly, this reunion can begin to heal our intergenerational trauma of the wounded feminine in our families. The reunification has the potential for us to heal the maternal wounds as we learn to see ourselves and each other with more depth and clarity. Daly speaks to this possibility:

> Radical feminism releases the inherent dynamic in the mother-daughter relationship toward friendship, which is strangled in the male-mastered system. Radical feminism means that mothers do *not* demand Self-sacrifice of daughters, and that daughters do not demand this of their mothers, as do sons in patriarchy. What both demand of each other is courageous moving which is mythic in its depths, which is spell-breaking and myth-making process.
>
> (39–40)

Recovering Athena's matrilineal seems to have been the symbolic expression that I have needed to see through my own relationship with my mother and father. With this new "vision," I could begin to find my way toward understanding what it means to stop asking my mother to "self-sacrifice," and to pull away from my projection of a perfect mother. This way I can enter into a new relationship with my mother, where she, too, stops demanding self-sacrifice from me. I have since been able to understand my own experiences in a way that Daly refers to as "seeing with our own eyes" into a world which excluded the feminine strength in my own story. I have felt oppressed by the patriarchal conditions imposed upon women, which, for me, were first experienced at home with my father (the training to devalue the feminine) at the expense of the emphasized value on logo-centric thinking and being. Far too often, while hearing my father's belittling remarks towards my mother, I believed them. Society trains us to take men's words at face value rather than question their intent and veracity. These experiences have contributed to creating a sense of alienation with myself and the world around me. Through telling Metis's story, we can re-member our mothers as we enact a recovery and resuscitation of the female bodies of knowledge, which constitute our matrilineal inheritance. Re-membering our mothers is a way to claim our *mêtis*, our inner wisdom.

Todas Las Madres

Figure 4.1 Author Clara Oropeza.
Photo by Mary Jane Cole.

Learning about my mother's life through her own gaze, along with the politics that shaped her, has given me greater depth into the woman that raised me (her resourcefulness, her wisdom and her own fallibilities). However, it has been a circuitous route to get me here, and, in essence, to go home. I first went off to college in search of substitute mothers, as I sought literary relationships that would nurture me. I continued to search for feminine images, mythic tropes, and poetic ways of being that have stayed with me ever since. And while it was my mother's silence, and my grandmother's unprocessed grief, that told me my life would have to be saved, it was Virginia Woolf and other Eurpoean literary figures whom I admire that taught me that my search was a yearning to find my own language. I sought refuge in the words of other writers, such as Hope Mirrless, Simone de Beauvoir, Colette and Mina Loy who helped me to examine the female condition as a path towards my own creative ambitions. I read fearlessness in their experiences about womanhood and the ways that women move toward creating a voice and authorial power of their own.

Years later, I would find the fateful words of Anaïs Nin, who concretely describes that writing was the "way out" in reference to how she felt after writing her first book. In an interview in 1972, Nin shared that "the first book I wrote then connected me with the vivacious literary life of Paris. It was the writing which was the way out" (Hinz, *A Woman Speaks* 225). For Nin, writing was the way out from the limiting psychological patterns that she knew she needed to make conscious for herself. Both Nin and Woolf were preoccupied with the importance of a female literary tradition for women writers. They both believed that writing our way out is what women do when we reimagine myths that have excluded a matrilineal lineage. Woolf's often quoted line resonated deeply with me: "a woman writing thinks back through her mothers" (*A Room of One's Own* 106). I began believing in my own iteration of this credo: writing our way out of patriarchal constraints happens also when we hear our mother's (figurative, literary and literal) stories flowing through our bodies, as we gain a new language of our own to feel and express who we are becoming. Nin and I share the same first language, Spanish. We both have Latina roots, experiences with navigating the oppressive social conditioning stemming from Catholicism, overpowering fathers, and we both were raised by mothers who were silenced by our fathers. Nin's vision added to what I had already learned from Woolf, while offering additional clues of artistic autonomy and literary models that I could rely on for myself.

Then came the time when I was learning to think critically about the world from the intersections of my identity as a Latina who grew up in a low-income household as a straight, cisgender woman in the academy.[9] While I attended college in the 1990s as an English major, there were few women of color who were part of the curriculum. BIPOC writers would eventually become available to me mostly through taking courses in other departments like Chicano Studies and Latin American Studies. That is where I finally discovered the voices of BIPOC women who had been left out of the canon of my early education, like bell hooks, Audre Lord, Toni Morrison, Cherríe Moraga, Gloria Anzaldúa, Sandra Cisneros, Joy Harjo, Leslie Marmon Silko and Sonia Sanchez, among others. In their works, book by book, I read about the realities that more mirrored my own. I read about diverse experiences not just with gender but intersections with race and social class. I heard the voices of women who, like me, navigated tensions stemming from racism and misogyny; and who knew what it meant to straddle two cultures and multiple languages in life. BIPOC feminists taught me how to think critically about my own material conditions and influences in my life, including the gaps in my education.

My new literary discoveries gave way to an inner tension. I began to realize the incongruity of my admiration of Woolf and other white literary figures; however, I grappled with an inability to name such tension. It slipped through my fingers, as I was unable to cradle its volatility. I knew its moods and textures that surfaced when I sat down to write: a tightness in my chest, a gray fog in my mind. I wondered, "was this the price for identifying so profoundly with white literary women? Who and what was telling me that identifying with white feminists was now unacceptable?" I began asking myself what many women of color eventually ask themselves: have I become too used to archetypal experiences depicted by white women? What does a first-genera- tion Mexican-American woman have in common with a Victorian English woman like Virginia Woolf, or with the other white women I was identifying with at the time?

In this sense, despite being of a different generation, I identified with bell hooks when she writes about becoming aware of the experiences that sepa- rated her from Emily Dickinson and Virginia Woolf. In "Zora Neale Hur- ston: A Subversive Reading," hooks writes:

> I never thought of Dickinson or Woolf as "white women." They entered the segregated world of my growing up as writers, and most importantly, as women writers. Later I would learn the distance separating their experience from my own, the politics of race, sex and class – still their work spoke to me.
>
> (hooks 174)

Gloria Anzaldúa reached a moment wherein she too saw through the material differences between her and Woolf's *A Room of One's Own*. Writing to women of color, Anzaldúa recommends: "Forget the room of one's own – write in the kitchen, lock yourself up in the bathroom. Write on the bus or the welfare line, on the job or during meals, between sleeping or waking" ("Speaking in Tongues" 168). I, too, had to learn a new way to let European feminists speak to me, while building my own language, beyond theirs.

The bigger question that came next seemed like a natural progression. Why had I left my ancestral mothers behind and out of my writing process? I rea- lized that I could not merely advocate for my own freedom. I also needed to tend to my wounds and heal the ways that the feminine in my family and cul- ture had been mistreated and misrepresented. I wondered why this was not previously possible. Was it due entirely to my *mis*-education? Or was it because I had found it psychologically and unwittingly difficult to stay and know the wounds of my own land, of my ancestral mothers and sisters, and all that was taken, and continues to be taken, from us? The risk to write about my own life felt too paramount to take on as I lacked the skills and confidence. I needed the creative courage to embrace the tensions, and at times, the chaotic field, that is the feminine side of the creative process. It would take me decades to gain courage. Along the way, I discovered in my writing that I needed to claim three domains of my existence, each with its own language and history: First, a canonical literary heritage that was gained through my education. Then the BIPOC voices that had largely been left out of my early education; and finally, my matrilineal inheritance. These realms, and others, inform my own creativity. Alice Walker presents an argument in *In Search of Our Mothers' Gardens*: for too long, women of color have relied on role models drawn from their (white- authored) education, instead of looking to their own mother's lives for inspiration. She argues, "we have constantly looked high, when we should have looked high – and low" (239). While Walker seems to refer to the idiom "searching high and low," in this context, she contrasts white writers from our education (high) with our mother's stories (low). In doing so, there is the potential to indicate that one form is superior to the other. Therefore, I propose the term "literary heritage," to represent the literary forebearers we acquire through our education (searching high), and the "maternal inheritance," meaning the voices found when rooting around close to the earth for our mother's and ancestral stories (searching low). Walker recognizes that for many of our mothers, who were consumed by surviving the perils of poverty and the patriarchy, the past has receded into the backdrop of their lives. Telling their stories was a luxury they could not afford because surviving was at the fore-front of their lives. As a result, what gets passed down in the silence is shame and trauma. Walker advocates that we locate, and write about, our own his-tories, including our mother's stories. By doing so, it will lead us toward a wellspring of creativity and a potential for healing the wounded matrilineal legacies in our lives.

As a woman of color, I understand the fact that there has been a colossal gap in my education, both of "literary heritage" and "maternal inheritance." It is, therefore, my desire and duty to bridge this gap through my own research and life experiences, including learning to listen to what is important to my soul. We must go deeper, and root around to know what needs to be claimed and to find an embodied language with which to express it. It is the same quest that Sandra Cisneros acknowledges when she remarks: "I'm on a mission to make up for the huge gaps in my miseducation as a woman of color." For me, this means forging through my own educational path, con-verging with a soul-search for the feminine sensibility that represents and speaks to my multifarious experiences. Alice Walker puts it this way:

> What is always needed in the appreciation of art, or life, is the larger per-spectives. Connections made, or at least attempted, where none existed before, the straining to encompass in one's glance at the varied world the common thread, the unifying theme through immense diversity, a fearlessness of growth, of search, of looking, that enlarges the private and the public world.
>
> (5)

I can hear Walker urging us to find ways to weave all parts of ourselves, even the ones that do not seem to belong. In the process of uniting the seemingly disparate parts of ourselves, we learn to trust the potential emerging patterns. In Walker's words, "it is in the end, the saving of lives that we writers are about ... We care because we know this: the life we save is our own" (14). Walker helps me better understand the source of the deep need I have to write: it is about tending psyche and about renewal. Engaging with the crea-tive process gives me a sense of liberation and the strength to carry on.

The Harder Work of Going Home

My mother's experiences with abandonment and shame have lived in the psychic history of my matrilineal heritage. Understanding my path towards healing my maternal wound has been a process of acknowledging that I had also internalized her shame into my own life. In *On Shame and the Search for Identity*, Helen Merrell Lynd writes: "Living in terms of the confronting of shame – and allowing shame to become a revelation of oneself and of one's society – makes way for living beyond the conventions of a particular culture" (257). Writing shame out of our personal narratives and balancing our bodies is a way to transcend shame and live beyond it. Confronting shame, Lynd writes, is also a recognition of "an integrity that is peculiarly one's own and of those characteristically human qualities that are at the same time most individualizing and most universal" (257). Throughout the interview process for writing her story (Chapter 3), my mother and I, together, identified the sources of our own shame within the Mexican and American cultural constructs. We reflected on the internalized patriarchal power structures imposed upon our own womanhood. Together, we acknowledged our personal experiences of this deeply human and archetypal emotion and of the familial politics behind it. While my survival burdens are different than those of my mother, together we found a new ability to endure our personal sufferings and truths. This allowed us to clear the pathway towards mending the intergenerational cycle of suffering that had afflicted our matrilineal legacy. By me asking questions, and through her openness to share her story, together we broke the cycle that had for generations passed down silence. Now, this interconnectivity has been the place from which we can connect to our intergenerational higher self, "a place of both self-enlightenment and ancestral enlightenment" (Buqué 29).

My mother's individuation story (Chapter 3), as she has recited it to me, has connected me to a legacy of strength and determination. Her story has been the missing foundation from which I could now move more deeply into my own healing. In telling and embodying her story through the intimate details of her life, my mother and I enacted an archetypal feminine way of being. We were brought together through our embodied longing to find and be guided by inner strength and admiration for feminine *fuerza* (strength). In telling her story, she was able to break the silences in which the patriarchal world had made her feel *asfixiada* (asphyxiated). By reorienting my sense of womanhood alongside my mother's, I have gained a deeper appreciation of our inter-beingness. With this newfound appreciation, I now confidently feel a deeper sense of myself as being a truly different and separate human being from my mother. In essence, this is the autonomy I have sought from her for years. Naturally, this new proximity, of course, invites a new psychological way of relating to her and her newly found happiness. Embedded in this discovery of tending my maternal wound is the possibility to make authentic connections with the unmothered parts within me. I can now begin to offer myself the inner security and love that I sought from her for most of my life. It is now possible to nurture a wholeness and to see a different internal guiding image of myself, no longer as the wounded and resentful daughter.

As my mother shared her *testimonio*, she spoke to me in tones that vacillated between anger, shame, sadness and finally, dignity. I intimately witnessed the strength that propelled her way beyond the thresholds of engulfing pain. By telling her story, my mother was able to regain her self-worth and her confidence. Together, by trusting the story-telling process, we reversed the narrative of her prior appearance of weakness. We realized that her perceptions of weakness were actually a story generated by the embedded structures of a patriarchal society, which was then amplified in the echo-chamber of our household, as ruled by my father. In those moments, together, we traveled toward an intimacy that had never been journeyed. For me, this was the long-awaited moment of acquiescence to grieve what no longer served us both, and to replace it with the possibilities of us creating a new relationship together. It was the kind of transformation that Galt Atlas describes in *Emotional Inheritance: A Therapist, Her Patients, and the Legacy of Trauma*. She writes: "The permission to grieve for our losses and faults, as well as for our parents', connects us with life and welcomes the birth of new possibilities" (112). Tending my own maternal wound cleared a path for my mother to also make her own wounds conscious.

My mother has relied on me to put into my own words what she has been yearning to claim: her de-shaming narrative, a modest memorial. Also, my mother's encouragement that I include her narrative in this collection is her way of advocating for the pivotal role that our stories hold for breaking old silences. Remembering also serves a purpose of releasing, and transcending the shame and fear, despite its grip upon the women in my family for far too long. Ultimately, my mother and I, together as two cartographers, re-mapped the shame that needed to be made visible.

The Personal as Political: Tending Our Mother's Mythos as a Way to Mend the Broken Web

As long as we continue living in a patriarchal ordered world, we will continue getting caught in the same broken web, and with the opportunities to heal our maternal wounds constantly being jeopardized. Moreover, without the intimacy that is created among us through the telling of our stories, we remain entangled in patriarchal distortions about ourselves and others. For many, the maternal wound runs too deep, and, in many cases, persistent sexism and racism continuously stalls and stunts healing. It is important to believe that when we tend to our own maternal wounds, opportunities for healing can open for others. We must support one another as we move through our unique individuation thresholds. The healing we do in our lives will not only deepen our relationships with the feminine essence of our own being, but it also links us to one another in a profound way. We must know that breaking the cycles of silence, trauma, and shame is a necessary path towards psychologically transforming the wounds bestowed upon the feminine psyche by the patriarchy, otherwise it will continue to be perpetuated through our matrilineal lineages.

As we consider the possibilities available to tending to intergenerational trauma, particularly the wounded feminine in our families, I think of Mariel Buqué's important work on the notion of being a cycle breaker. In *Break the Cycle: A Guide to Healing Intergenerational Trauma*, Buqué writes that cycle breaking is "how we put down that baggage of the past and step into a better future. Cycle breakers *choose* to be cycle breakers. It is an active, long-term decision" (13). I contend that we land on the necessity to be a cycle breaker by following our intuition that relationships in our family must change. The wounds must be made visible so that they may be given proper healing and closure. Also, it is my conviction that to be a cycle breaker, one must trust in the ancient healing power of stories. "Being a cycle breaker is a multitier, multitask, multigenerational quest towards acquiring peace. It's peace for you, those who came before you, those who will come after you, your community, and the global culture," writes Buqué (14). We all can make the strides and contributions towards breaking the cycles of trauma in our families. By choosing to turn toward, and honoring, the stories of our matrilineal legacies, we disrupt the inflicted cycles of pain upon the feminine essence in our lives. We can begin by doing the inner work necessary to acknowledge our individual pain and re-map how it got there, in order to move towards self-forgiveness and collective healing. Buqué moves onto write that recognition of our power to be and see ourselves as a "living ancestor who has influence over future generations," is a move toward ending the cycle of inherited trauma (15).

As we know, cultural and societal messaging is first transmitted within our families. Therefore, our families are also the location from which we can affect great change. The link between the personal and the political is what Mary Wollstonecraft had in mind centuries ago when, in her essay "A Vindication of the Rights of Woman," she wrote: "A man has been termed a microcosm and every family might also be called a state" (374). Wollstonecraft astutely points out that our families are the initial microcosms to shape our life values, constructs and politics. These influences are then expanded to represent one's own self within the world outside our homes, which still holds true today. The action required to better understand our mothers' mythos, the stories which comprise the rich and multifaceted lives they have lived, is a collective matter. How we are taught to mistrust and disrespect the feminine in our own families must be examined.

Undoubtedly, there must be a conscious recognition of how toxic the patriarchal dominance is upon our families and our culture at large. When this profound imbalance is created, it leads to the feminine becoming alienated in all of us. Paradoxically, when our mothers are swallowed and daughters are disrespected and marginalized, the stories of our fathers and sons also get lost. Fortunately, everyone can participate in re-visioning and understanding the value of a matrilineal inheritance of one's own. Examining the politics in our own families, including how they play out in our personal relationships, allows us to cultivate a feminine sensitivity and willingness to take restorative actions so that we may all benefit.

Notes

1 In "Dancing with Mystery," I use the myth of Persephone and Demeter to explore my complex relationship with my mother.
2 My mother was 82 years old when I began interviewing her for what would be Chapter 3 of this book.
3 My father opened his own roofing company when I was thirteen. His work as a *techero* (roofer) began when he was 20 years old and newly immigrated to the United States. For the first decade that he worked as a roofer, OSHA did not exist. And for the nearly fifty years that he was in this line of work, the industry was mostly unregulated. For a vast part of the time he was an employee, roofers were not unionized. The potential for a life-threatening incident, from a wide variety of occupational hazards – the most common of which stemmed from working with, and breathing in, hot tar – was a daily occurrence. Working without respiratory protection from toxic materials like asbestos, and no fall protection, were other hazards of this line of work.
4 In fact, C.G. Jung and Anaïs Nin both said it: when we dive into the personal content of our psyche, and dwell in it long and deep enough, we touch the archetypal.
5 See "Metis, Mêtis, Mestiza, Medusa: Rhetorical Bodies across Rhetorical Traditions," wherein Jay Dolmage argues that the myth of the Greek goddess Metis offers critical insights for how to restore embodied intelligence into rhetorical theory and history.
6 The Titans are the pre-Olympian gods, including the sisters Thea, Rhea, Themis, Mnemosyne, Phoebe, and Tethys. The brothers are Oceanus, Coeus, Crius, Hyperion, Iapetus and Cronos.
7 Zeus's siblings include Hera, Hades, Poseidon and Hestia.
8 Daly's work reminds us that as we move further on the "Metapatriarchal journey," we find deeper and deeper layers of these pernicious patterns embedded in the culture, implanted in our souls (8).
9 In 1989 Kimberlé Crenshaw coined the term intersectionality to describe the places where our social categories (race, gender, sexuality, ability, class) overlap and shape our experiences.

References

Anzaldúa, Gloria. *Borderlands/La Frontera*. San Francisco. Aunt Lute Books. 1999.
Anzaldúa, Gloria. "Speaking in Tongues: A Letter to Third World Women Writers." *This Bridge Called My Back*. Albany. Suny Press. 2015.
Apollodorus. *The Library*. Loeb Classical Library Volumes 121 and 122. Trans. Sir James George Frazer. Cambridge, MA. Harvard University Press. 1921.
Atlas, Galt. *Emotional Inheritance: A Therapist, Her Patients, and the Legacy of Trauma*. London. Little, Brown. 2022.

Baring, Ann and Jules Cashford. *The Myth of the Goddess: Evolution of an Image.* New York. Penguin Books. 1991.

Buqué, Mariel. *Break the Cycle: A Guide to Healing Intergenerational Trauma.* New York. Dutton. 2024.

Cisneros, Sandra. "Sandra Cisneros Loves to Read About Women Waging Battle." *New York Times*, September 5, 2021. Retrieved from www.nytimes.com/2021/09/02/books/review/sandra-cisneros-by-the-book-interview.html.

Cori, Jasmine Lee. *The Emotionally Absent Mother. How to Recognize and Heal the Invisible Effects of Childhood Emotional Neglect.* New York. The Experiment. 2017.

Crenshaw, Kimberlé. "Kimberlé Crenshaw on Intersectionality, More than Two Decades Later." June 8, 2017. Retrieved from www.law.columbia.edu/news/archive/kimberle-crenshaw-intersectionality-more-two-decades-later.

Daly, Mary. *Gyn/Ecology: The Metaethics of Radical Feminism.* Boston. Beacon Press. 1990.

Dolmage, Jay. "Metis, Mêtis, Mestiza, Medusa: Rhetorical Bodies across Rhetorical Traditions." *Rhetoric Review* 28(1) (2009): 1–28.

Downing, Christine. *The Goddess: Mythological Images of the Feminine.* New York. The Crossroad Publishing Company. 1988.

Gómez-Cano, Grisel. *The Return to Coatlicue: Goddesses and Warladies in Mexican Folklore.* Bloomington, IN. Xlibris Corporation. 2010.

Harrison, Jane. *Prolegomena to the Study of Greek Religion.* New York. World Publishing Company. 1959.

Hillman, James. *Re-visioning Psychology.* New York. Harper & Row. 1975.

Hinz, Evelyn J. *A Woman Speaks: The Lectures, Seminars, and Interviews of Anaïs Nin.* Chicago. The Swallow Press. 1975.

hooks, bell. "Zora Neale Hurston: A Subversive Reading." *Remembered Rapture: The Writer at Work.* New York. Henry Holt and Company. 1999.

Kaufman, Gershen. *Shame: The Power of Caring.* Rochester, VT. Schenkman Books. 1992.

Léger, Nathalie. *The White Dress.* London. Les Fugitives. 2020.

Levy, Deborah. *Hot Milk.* London. Bloomsbury. 2017.

Lynd, Helen Merrell. *On Shame and the Search for Identity.* New York. Harcourt, Brace and Company. 1958.

Moraga, Cherríe. *Native Country of the Heart.* New York. Farrar, Straus and Giroux. 2019.

Phillips, Shelley. *Beyond the Myths: Mother–Daughter Relationships in Psychology, History, Literature and Everyday Life.* London. Penguin Books. 1991.

Sieff, D. F. "Confronting Death Mother: An Interview with Marion Woodman." *The Psychology of Violence: A Journal of Archetype and Culture* Spring 81 (2009): 177–199.

Viramontes, Helena Maria. *The Moths and Other Stories.* Houston. Arte Público Press. 1995.

Walker, Alice. *In Search of Our Mothers' Gardens.* New York. Harcourt. 1983.

Wollstonecraft, Mary. "A Vindication of the Rights of Woman: With Strictures on Political and Moral Subjects." *The Norton Anthology of Literature by Women: The Traditions in English.* 3rd edition. Ed. Sandra M. Gilbert and Susan Gubar. New York. W. W. Norton & Company. 2007.

Woolf, Virginia. *A Room of One's Own.* London. Hogarth Press. 1929.

Chapter 5

Seasons of My Discontent

Fall/Winter

It was mid-autumn and the days were short. It was in the early stages of identifying the direction of this work when I contended with sharp pain emanating from my sacrum and hips. All the muscles and tendons in the surrounding areas: glutes, hips and sacrum area, tightened as I slowly walked about the world in a tense, protectively posed, mis-aligned body. I was forced to pull back from my regular physical activities –no barre classes, no garden projects. The only walking I could do was by taking micro steps, as if there were torsion springs inside of me, forcing me to walk like a wound-up toy. I wondered what my bones were trying to whisper to me. It was the perfect metaphor for where I was in my writing, so I knew I could not overlook that my body and my book were in a symbiotic relation. And so, writing was in some ways a journey (rite of passage) of realigning my body.

I experienced the onset of physical symptoms, which I would later realize were a manifestation of the deep psychological shifts that would occur throughout the writing process of this work. The country was abiding the stay-at-home orders due to COVID, limiting my treatment options. I had no official prognosis, but at this point I could not help but wonder if this was something out of the opening passage in Anaïs Nin's novelette *House of Incest*:

> The morning I got up to begin this book I coughed. Something was coming out of my throat: it was something strangling me. I broke the thread which held it and yanked it out. I went back to bed and said: I have just spat out my heart.
>
> (11)

Nin knew that writing is an act that moves through and enlists the body, sweeping up emotional truths that our narratives need to make sense.

My body and mood were overtaken by fatigue, and the attention this pain was drawing to myself made me hyper self-conscious, as if the version of self-consciousness I already embodied is not enough of an adversary to my

DOI: 10.4324/9781003255857-5

writing. The pain waxed and waned throughout the day. On most mornings, my greatest hope was that I could sit up and summon the concentration to read a book, where the pain could coil up into someone else's words, losing its tight grip on my body. During this time, I began organizing the ideas for my book proposal. I began to store scantily written files in my laptop with titles like: "Book Proposal Ideas" and "Introduction Outline."

The ideas I wanted to write about encircled the lives and works of remarkable modernist women who had preoccupied my imagination, such as Anaïs Nin, Simone de Beauvoir, Victoria Ocampo, Virginia Woolf and Gabriela Mistral. Broadly, I was interested in studying the link between creativity and individuation, and how the two are shaped or undermined by intersections of gender, class and race. I wanted to make connections between modernist women writing in Europe and South America during the same historical time. Then the deeper I got into the topic, the more I began to feel haunted by the fact that I had drawn inspiration only from a literary matrilineal lineage, and not from my biological maternal line.

As I searched for the right vessel for my ideas, my dreams were peppered with images of me in Paris's Left Bank where, under a silver-gray sky – in an unhurried pace – I wove in and out of Anglophone bookstores. In each, I inventoried bookshelf after bookshelf in search of a book that seemed to be nonexistent. This dream led me to query what book it was that I so urgently needed to read. That is when I realized that the work I needed to write had to include my matrilineal line, not just my literary mothers. It was Toni Morrison who once said that the impetus for her novels was that she wrote the books she needed to read (Morrison 11). So, here I was, finding out what book I needed to read, by way of knowing that I needed to author it. But first I needed to find the linking narrative connections that would add fluidity to my story, like pearls on a silk thread. I recalled that asking the right questions is a critical part of the individuation process.

I began to wonder if writing solely about the literary figures I had been so drawn to in my academic life had kept me from a deeper search and an understanding of the wounds of my own land, embodied by my ancestral mothers. In her powerful memoir *Native Country of the Heart*, Cherríe Moraga describes her experience with this tension:

> For all my feminism, this is why I left a white women's movement in the late 1970s. So I wouldn't have to explain anymore, translate anymore. Because translating, I knew, would keep me from the harder work of going home …
>
> (4)

Similarly, my book, I was beginning to realize, was being propelled by a deep desire to capture into words the stories of my maternal line. In this sense, guided by the language of my literary mothers, I now needed to learn that of my own maternal line, and re-map my path towards home: of trying to find the language to help me understand – within the context of my gender and culture – how I could claim my own voice.

Spring

In early spring, while the pink Eden roses in our garden were beginning to bloom, as I got closer to solidifying my book topic, the pain intensified in my coccyx. The discomfort made it so that sitting for long periods of time sent piercing pain through my sacrum. I could no longer reach for and lift Emma, my 15-pound terrier. I started physical therapy after getting my COVID vaccination. Each week at physical therapy, and at night at home with my husband, I grappled in an anti-narrative state to describe the location, intensity and actual feeling of the acute pain taking over all other reality. It never failed, as I set out to find the words to describe this subterranean geography that only I was experiencing, my mind leapt instead onto the pages of Elaine Scarry's meditation on the vulnerability of the human body, as she writes about in *The Body in Pain: The Making and Unmaking of the World.* I agree with her premise: pain – as an interior state – has "no referential context" to the outside world (5). There is no pain of, or pain for, as used to describe other interior states; therefore, it remains certain only to the one experiencing it (5). She writes, "while for the other person it is so elusive that 'hearing about pain' may exist as the primary model of what it is to 'have doubt'" (4). This means that pain is something un-sharable that both "cannot be denied and that which cannot be confirmed" (4). I lived in this liminality of expression of my pain, while I searched for the sentences to also describe the book that was germinating in me.

At the same time, I was preoccupied with ways to return to my ancestral lands, to retrieve the stories of the life of a prominent woman in my family, my mother. I wondered about the emotional landscapes that my mother, her mother, and her mother's mother had traveled. The questions that were starting to animate me were around the topic of how we learn to have the courage to come into our own, including how we learn to claim our creative will as women. What role do our mothers play in our individuation, and in supporting our access to our own creativity? I began to be reassured by my literary mothers (Gloria Anzaldúa, Cherríe Moraga, Anaïs Nin, Sor Juana Inés de la Cruz, Alice Walker, Virginia Woolf, among others) and through research that going in search of a matrilineal heritage is archetypal. I recognized that this archetypal search must be the core topic of this book. Psychically, I was tapping into what it means to be on the path towards individuation, alongside our mothers and to seek community with our sisters. I knew that I was not the first one to have this impulse. The poet Audre Lorde reminds us that "there are no new ideas. There are only new ways of making them felt, of examining what our ideas really mean ..." (2). I wanted to examine what it felt like to dwell on the archetypal nature of searching for a matrilineal line, as a path toward calling forth inner feminine knowing and healing. I was curious of the various patterns of experiences, behaviors and paths towards greater inner wisdom that support and expand our voices and stories.

During this time, in my dreams, I often found myself in unidentifiable dark city streets. Another theme was that my wallet was stolen, so I was robbed of an acceptable form of identifying myself to others. It seemed that psyche agreed that I was traversing new territory, new dark city streets, wherein I would have to mine my own resources to gain access to a fresh identity that was unfolding. Also, during this time, I had a reoccurring dream that I was steering my own, one-person, boat from one shoreline, across a large body of water, to another. Since boats represent voyaging, and there I was alone, the image suggested where I was in life: crossing a threshold, in liminality toward another world. I was indeed between worlds. This reoccurring dream resonated with me as an individuation journey, as I was voyaging (in my writing), crossing worlds, endeavoring to become aware of the matrilineal lineages (literary and personal) that had shaped me.

Summer

At the height of "May – gray" in Santa Barbara, while dense fog hovered for most of the day – my book ideas were organized into a twelve-page proposal. While I knew the topics I was interested in exploring, I would have to be patient while the creative process unfolded and other themes emerged. Just then, I felt my life contracting as I was faced with the reality that my sixteen-year-old canine companion and creative partner, Emma, was needing extra care and medical attention. She suffered from an enlarged heart, a heart murmur and severe arthritis. She was the one life I had mothered all these years. For the past fourteen years, Emma and I had shared life's adventures and perils. I knew I would have to face the blatant fact that she was not long for this material world. But how? Her fragile heart failure was real, whether I could experience it as reality or not. Death, I learned, will loom and stay until it takes what it has come to claim.

My body continued contracting, specifically in my hips: they had little to no range of motion, and I could hardly make any lateral movements with my legs. An oddly short stride made it painful to walk. The backs of my glute muscles and my IT band were now as solid as concrete. When I got little to no relief from physical therapy, I moved on to work with a chiropractor.

In the Chiropractor's Office

The chiropractor walked through the long corridor where colorful framed images of bronze Buddhas, local Santa Barbara ocean landscapes, and pink lotus flowers covered the lavender-painted walls. Before looking at my patient folder, including my eight-page new patient questionnaire I had labored over minutes earlier, the chiropractor, in her straight posture, with beach blonde curls flying past her shoulders, called me by my first name. Impressed, and relieved by this warm gesture, I did what she asked: "follow me to the open door at the end of the hallway."

Along with the standard questions I had been asked during other initial doctor's appointments, here I heard one I hadn't before: "What do *you* believe is wrong with you?" I wanted to tell her that what I feared most was that the untangling of my book ideas was toying with my vertebrae, as the ground underneath me churned. I seemed to be descending into the spirit of the feminine that had been wounded and thus dormant in my life. I wanted to tell her that I was trying to give voice to the stories of my ancestors, so their unprocessed grief could stop the symbolic deaths from happening. I wanted to tell her that what I feared was that the restrictions I felt from not having the language and confidence to write, was like the way that my skeletal system was holding me back from moving freely in my body. I wanted to tell her about my heart's attachment to an aging canine-daughter of fourteen years, who was slipping away toward death. However, there was also the version that had to do with a slip I had had off a ladder six months earlier. I decided to tell her both stories, and let her decide which one she could best treat.

After completing a series of muscle tests on both my right and left side, the chiropractor declared that three areas needed adjustments: hip, pubic and L5 were my "problems." She requested I "lay down facing forward." She adjusted my left hip and L5 by gently, but sharply, pressing on them with her bare hands. I lay on the treatment table, breathing deeply into my belly, as I hoped that the sound of my own deep breathing would infuse re-alignment into my body. Nearly simultaneously, when the chiropractor's index finger sent a sharp press through the right-side of my pubic bone, grief was released and exited my body in the form of tears. A stream of tears dashed towards my temples, and onto the cold polyvinyl treatment table. This went on for minutes and, as if knowing it was useless to hold back the tears, I did not stop myself from allowing grief to move through me. And in this order, my treatment unfolded: bones pressed, streams of tears released. It is said that we carry grief in our hips.

As I began mapping the landscapes of my literary and ancestral mothers for my book, one thing was certain. I would need to take inventory of my newly excavated relic: grief. I would have to analyze, log, and map its function, origins, shape, and size. I must describe its attributes, including the material conditions it is made of. The more I sought to untangle its tendrils, the thicker and faster the grief grew, wrapping itself around every sub-topic that I sought to re-map.

Gaining access to my own voice meant that I was coming to terms with something that had profoundly been denied to the women in my matrilineal line. I was coming to realize that the grief I was accessing was enveloped in a sense of loss for the mother that I (and my ancestral mothers), scarcely, if at all, had emotional access to, living in a patriarchal world. My interest in womanhood and creativity resonates with what Sylvia Brinton Perera writes about in her book *Descent to the Goddess: A Way of Initiation for Women.* She poignantly notes:

> Unfortunately, all too many modern women have not been nurtured by the mother in the first place. Instead, they have grown up in the difficult home of abstract, collective authority... [o]r they have identified with the father and their patriarchal culture, thus alienating themselves from their own feminine ground and the personal mother, whom they have often seen as weak or irrelevant.
>
> (7)

My own alienation from a "feminine ground and [my] personal mother" would have to be at the center. The search for the matrilineal, I was realizing, had to include confronting not only my own grief, but also that of my female ancestors, who many had been abused and unprotected, and themselves had not been mothered. My longing to identify with a matrilineal heritage – to re-map my own – had placed me at a threshold onto a path of my own individuation. I was learning to tend to my own grief along the way. This included the need to remember the wounds of my childhood that related to having felt emotionally abandoned by my mother. I started to believe that for many of us, by claiming our matrilineal line, we gain support for the inner work we must also do to tend the negative masculine that stems from our experiences with domineering fathers. That work can then be approached with feminine strength, which we are capable of recovering.

Late summer arrived, bearing warmer sea temperatures, along with it a weight that, while somewhat expected, loaded my heart anew: Emma's health had further declined. It was time to let her go and fulfill her life cycle. During the last week of her life, my husband and I created a hospice environment for her. We lit white candles, read her poetry and filled the living room with Eden roses from our garden. In Buddhism it is known that the love with which one is surrounded at the end of life, is the love with which the soul will enter its next life. We wanted to send her off enveloped in pure love. Her canine world had grown mine into places of wonder and love unlike I had previously experienced. Her love had expanded me, and now the thought of her absence resulted in a visceral contraction of my entire body. I walked into the void, a blueish darkness that tugged at me wherever I went for months. The anxieties that I carried about my daily life were now nestled into a grieving heart. I felt my heart contracting, getting smaller, protecting what I had already lost.

I recall the depiction of the closeness one gains to a beloved canine companion as tenderly captured by the narrator in *The Friend*, by Sigrid Nunez. The narrator discovers that Apollo, the grieving dog she has taken custody of, likes to be read to. She writes: "He relaxes his head onto his paws, tipping his eyes at me each time I turn a page. The position of his ears shifts in response to my vocal inflections" (133). The two companions build intimacy through books. Similarly, I always saw Emma as a canine genius who too knew the value of words and of the solitude necessary to create. When I needed to write – to be in my writing room – it was as if she could sense the moment. Simultaneously, as I stood up from the dining chair in preparation to walk to my writing room, she arose from her bed, wagging her small tail and watching me, ready to join. I always got a sense that she was calmed by being in my writing room with me. As I sat in my desk chair, she relaxed in her beige teacup bed, with her small head softly resting on the rim, her brown eyes gazing straight at me.

Living through the unyielding heat of hot flashes radiating throughout my body, it was time to confront my own grief burning at my heart. It was as if the grief that I had previously not allowed to be fully expressed by way of processing it, was now resurfacing, asking to be tended. In *All About Love*, bell hooks reminds us that:

> in its deepest sense, grief is a burning of the heart, an intense heat that gives us solace and release. When we deny the full expression of our grief, it lays like a weight on our hearts, causing emotional pain and physical ailments.

> (201)

This passage reminded me that processing grief is also a path towards self-compassion, love and joy, all paradoxical feelings we are not meant to think of as part of grief. I knew that for my entire life, grief and fear have lived at my root, overwhelming me. Now, facing menopause, grief had a different flavor. It had an unrecognizable lightness to it because I was different. I could fully surrender to grieving Emma as a maternal process, honoring and recognize that in Emma's presence, I had touched a form of love that grounded me in knowing and trusting that love prevails over fear.

Fall/Winter

In September, my book proposal was accepted. It was official. I would be writing this book (that you are reading). The days were clear, fog and rain free, and my body required fewer and fewer chiropractic adjustments. That week, I had another repeated dream involving a boat and an ocean crossing. I was on a small, one-person boat, but this time, on my way towards a larger boat occupied by a full crowd of people. The waking feeling was that I, in my individual boat, would be joining a group of people who journey by boat across the sea. I could not help but wonder if the vessel with which I would be gathering with a community would be my book.

Spring

The following late Spring I began interviewing my mother about her life. Our first interview took place at the open-air courtyard of Mercado San Agustíne, under a perfect blue Tucson sky, as we sat across from one another under the shade of mesquite trees. I began by asking about her early years. Together, in our conversation, we traveled through rural Mexico where her memories live. Together we unearthed tender memories, wounds and possibilities. And in this way, silences were lifted. As I met new facets of her being, my own consciousness grew, as my heart softened. There sitting across from me, was a woman I had known all my life, yet never really knew the web of stories about her womanhood. She shared narratives of a woman who had not been mothered by her own mother, abandoned and shamed by men in her life. I learned about her unfulfilled dreams to go to cosmetology school and to own her own beauty salon. Then, later, she would have liked to return to school to study psychology (careers that two of her daughters would pursue). There was a woman who had for nearly thirty years been married to a man who disrespected and emotionally abused her. I came to understand how to better read the clouded eyes that bore the weight of a lifetime of unprocessed grief and trauma, stemming from having grown up in poverty. Her openness to my queries about her life gave way to a new ocean of intimacy between us, and within ourselves.

Writing has been an act of healing, like setting bones in their proper places. Returning to some of my life's pivotal moments, to grieve and remember alongside my personal mother, supported by literary mothers, has put me into dialogue with a new part of myself. I hear Virginia Woolf's wisdom speaking to me about the role of finding the right words to give "shocks," meaning, through writing. In the process of discovering what belongs where (like aligning vertebrae), a form of "wholeness" ensues. Woolf says it so brilliantly:

> I think this is true, because though I still have the peculiarity that I receive these sudden shocks, they are now always welcome; after the first surprise, I always feel instantly that they are particularly valuable. And so I go on to suppose that the shock-receiving capacity makes me a writer. It is only by putting it into words that I make it whole; this wholeness means that it has lost its power to hurt me; it gives me, perhaps because by doing so I take away the pain, a great delight to put the severed parts together. Perhaps this is the strongest pleasure known to me. It is the rapture I get when in writing I seem to be discovering what belongs to what.

> (*Moments of Being* 72)

Woolf seems to be speaking to the things that deepen individuation: being in creative conversation with the experiences that "shock" us, that send deep and thunderous waves through our being, deepening our "shock – receiving capacity" (72). To individuate demands that we become conscious by "discovering what belongs to what" (72). Woolf reminds us that writing brings consciousness onto the page, a way to "take away the pain" (72). It became apparent to me that re-aligning my body was intertwined with tending grief. I had to give it a proper resting place through the process of writing. I knew I would need to tap into the unacknowledged sorrows of my ancestors – that had been silenced for generations – that had been carried in the psyches and bodies of the women that came before me. It was this kind of tending that I wanted to ground me, so that I could find my voice. In writing this book, I vowed to not deny my own grief. Instead, I would trust it as worthy of love and attention, as in the sacred work of supporting my own body.

Summer

Re-mapping the crossings where my life intersects with a matrilineal line has been an embodied endeavor. I understand now that the pain that seized my body at the start of this writing project was my body preparing me to move into a new territory where consciousness expands, new energy arises, and new beginnings emerge. I am reminded of Sylvia Brinton Perera's notion that the "inner connection" to the self, the archetype of wholeness, is "an initiation essential for women in the Western world … the process requires both a sacrifice of our identity as spiritual daughters of the patriarchy …" (7–8). Re-mapping my own freedom has, all along, been a way toward surrendering myself to the process of claiming a matrilineal line, repositioning my body, from identifying solely as a daughter of the patriarchy. I have crawled out of the caverns of dark agony over having been disconnected from the power and passion of my matrilineal lineage, including locating my mother's untold story as an inspiring and enriching link to my own creative life. My desire to write this work, I realized, was less about an analysis of the lives of Simone de Beauvoir, Victoria Ocampo and Gabriela Mistral and more about learning how to trust in myself to write the personal stories that were asking to intersect with the broader topics in this book. The new psychic reality I have touched, through writing, came to me in a dream image at the completion stage of the manuscript:

> *I enter a dark portal, and I hear my own voice saying I can make the descent. I tell myself that I can continue traveling down through the darkness. I keep going. After a few moments, an image of my grandmother is released, as if ejected from a treasure chest that was buried deep in the sea of my body. And as I watch her float into space, like an astronaut, my mother's body then floats out of my sea-body, as if also being ejected from my chest, heart, and torso.*

I understood the image of the passing bodies as a psychic release of my maternal projections and intergenerational trauma. The dark portal I traveled through was the birth canal from which I transpired a new sense of myself.

Reaching a new proximity to my maternal wound, and having recognized how it contributed to my sense of womanhood, I now have the courage to keep the creative portal open. This way, I have access to the crossings I am meant to continue moving through, the opposite of stasis. Finding a matrilineal lineage has been about locating a feeling of orientation from where I can draw creative self-empowerment, a place wherein I could declare my own *métis*. With this, I am more attuned to Her, the Great Mother's, subtleties and possibilities for transformation, including her voice in nature.

References

hooks, bell. *All About Love: New Visions.* New York. HarperCollins. 2000.

Lorde, Audre. "Poetry is Not a Luxury." 1985. Retrieved from https://makinglearning. wordpress.com/wp-content/uploads/2014/01/poetry-is-not-a-luxury-audre-lorde.pdf.

Moraga, Cherríe. *Native Country of the Heart.* New York. Farrar, Straus and Giroux. 2019.

Morrison, Toni. *Toni Morrison: The Last Interviews and Other Conversations.* Brooklyn. Melville House. 2020.

Nin, Anaïs. *The House of Incest.* Athens. Swallow Press. 1958.

Nunez, Sigrid. *The Friend.* New York. Riverhead Books. 2018.

Perera, Sylvia Brinton. *Descent to the Goddess: A Way of Initiation for Women.* Toronto. Inner City Books. 1981.

Scarry, Elaine. *The Body in Pain: The Making and Unmaking of the World.* Oxford. Oxford University Press. 1985.

Woolf, Virginia. *Moments of Being: A Collection of Autobiographical Writing.* New York. Harcourt. 1985.

Epilogue
Cartography of the Feminine Gaze

My mother read the final draft of her chapter while visiting me in late summer. She read through each page carefully and quietly, holding a blue felt pen in her hand. Captivated in the narration of her life story, she recognized her life anew. Handing me her chapter, with her body soft and her voice forceful, she acknowledged, "I *have* lived a life worth telling." She went on to express that there were many themes in her story that she hoped would be relatable to readers. She spoke with a new sense of empowerment, as she expressed hope that her story would invite deeper conversations about womanhood and paths towards freedom. It was a new side of my mother that I had been getting to know throughout the interview process to write her chapter. It was the part of her that spoke of women's rights, of claiming her strength to build her own life, despite having been made to feel small her entire life.

Later, during the same visit she handed me a dossier containing her handwritten story from which my chapter draws. It was a grey writing pad containing her penmanship in black ink. On various pages, writing spills onto the margins; on some pages, small arrows direct the reader to the backside of the page. On the front page sits an inscription (Figure 6.1), which translates as follows:

> Dear Daughter, Clara,
>   Here I give you these pages that contain part of my life. I entrust them to you because I know that you will make good use of them. May God hope that everything turns out well for you and that you will soon be able to write the book we planned together.
>   With much respect and love,
>   Mom

As I consider what went into writing my mother's story in this work and the role that stories, and storytellers, have in supporting the complex ways that women step more fully into our own lives, I am reminded of *The White Dress* by Nathalie Léger. In *The White Dress*, Léger braids together stories about two women's struggles to find their liberation. One woman is the Italian

DOI: 10.4324/9781003255857-6

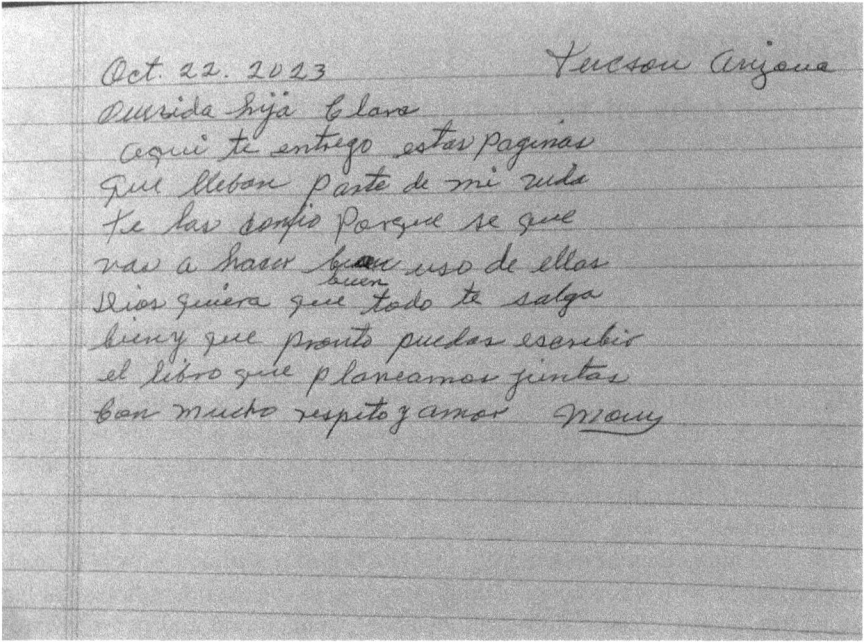

Figure 6.1 Inscription on my mother's notebook page.

performance artist Pippa Bacca. In March 2008, Pippa set out on "Bride on Tour," a journey through Eastern European and Middle Eastern countries to promote peace and union between people and the nations that have been torn by war.[1] The other woman in the story is Léger's mother. The first segment of the book is about her mother and the book ends with Pippa's story.

Early in the book, Léger's mother takes out a dossier containing the court documents detailing the dissolution of her marriage to her ex-husband, Léger's father. He took her to court, where public grievances were "levelled against her" (111). She was humiliated and charged with "maternal failings" (111). The dossier has the secondary material necessary to write her mother's own version of the story, which is blatantly absent from the court documents. Léger's mother has a deep yearning to have her story be told. This is a source of tension between mother and daughter because initially, Léger is hesitant to write about family history. Her mother pleads:

I've thought a lot about it, your two subjects are exactly the same, so you can help me, support me, assist me in my project at the same time as you're pursuing yours, because, … the violence is the same, great or small; whatever form it takes, the fight to denounce it… you can act in my name, you can speak for me… you can defend me or even avenge me

(7)

Léger's mother sees a symbolic connection between her life and the violence committed on Pippa, a victim of male sexual violence. Pippa was killed outside of Istanbul while on her "Bride Tour," while attempting to use her art to make an impact on society.[2]

Léger's mother equates her own suffering to that of Pippa. Each are victims of injustices under insidious patriarchal structures that demean women. Both result in death, be it actual or symbolic. She sees the urgency of telling stories to "denounce" the violence, "great or small," that is necessary to "defend" women's liberation, and to memorialize both women equally: a woman who has lost her life while seeking her own artistic freedom, and a woman who has lost her dignity in court and in her life (7). Léger is called to be her mother's *vindex*, "a protector, a defender, someone who demands compensation for reputational damage, the person who, in a word, repairs ..." (31). A mother chooses her daughter to carry out her justice, to tell her side of the story.

The conditions under which I initially arrived at my mother's story are indeed the inverse of Léger's. Her story was not pressed upon me; instead, I asked to be its vessel. For a long time, I knew that if her story got lost, then a part of mine would too. At the onset of this work, I sought insights into the attachments that keep us from accessing a deeper feminine existence that strips us of the courage to live our lives to the fullest, including sharing our art with the world. I approached my mother because her life deserved the same inquiry as my other academic interests. And while my scholarly training especially helped me shoulder my mother's suffering and the details of her private life while writing her chapter, it was through the drafting process that I was able to pull back judgment (one draft at a time), and in its place invite her life story to reveal itself. With each draft, reasons for being who she was emerged.

Then there is the question of how I managed the dark details that I learned involving my father. Some of the details I discovered made it so that, at times, I had to create some distance between my father and me, until I could emotionally process them. When I did resume contact with him, I found myself casually referring to some of the stories I had recently heard from my mother's perspective. I felt myself slipping into a query mode, not to pit his version against hers, but to experience how it felt in my body to have him confirm the truths I now knew. I began to recognize how liberating it was to have multiple narratives of the same events, which had previously been told solely from his masculine consciousness – he who had been reared to demand a female partner to attend to his needs. He is no longer the author of our family's official story. My queries were subtle, as neither one of us seemed to be off kilter in those moments. Instead, I felt a churning inside of me, like a tiller moving soil, as if the stories inside of me were being both separated, then re-mixed into a fresh layer of earth. Each story felt like it positioned me differently in the masculine-validated world in which I had been raised. Also, viewing my mother's life through her own gaze has meant that I no longer see my father as the oppressor. This new perspective into my mother, father and family *herstory* allows me to be more compassionate towards both of my parents, and the injustices they each have survived.

As her testimony is complete, Léger's mother tells her to go on and complete the original story she set out to write, her story about Pippa. The concluding section of *The White Dress* contains some of the most harrowing details of Pippa's tragic fate. At this point in the story, the reader can infer that after hearing (and writing) her mother's story, Léger taps into a newly found strength to continue with the last segment that concludes *The White Dress*. Pippa's murderer "raped her, he killed her, he stripped her naked and finally he stole her gaze" (115). He takes her camera, the one Pippa was using to document her trip, and records his niece's wedding. In the end, he turns the lens on himself (119).

In *The White Dress*, the description of the writer's role in supporting the female gaze and challenging oppression is stated by Léger's mother: "It's just about getting some form of redress," she states (101). Léger responds, "yes, this is what writing can do, adjust, blindly adjust, it's not much, but it's key" (102). Writing women's stories is a way to insist on our point of view being told, our humanity shared. Our stories force society to see us. We re-claim our gaze as we create solidarity. By restoring my own vantage point, I have "adjust[ed]" the lens, and thus inspired hope on the pathway towards healing the wounded feminine in my matrilineal line. While my inquiry into mother and daughter relationships is written primarily from the daughter's perspective, we know that the stories about these relationships are ever more complex. What these stories show about our mothers' influences on our lives and the tender and sorrowful rite of passage of becoming autonomous from them, is that our emotional ties to them, for many of us, are continuously evolving our connection to the feminine imagination.

By re-mapping the pivotal stages in the process of claiming their potential, in the lives of Anaïs Nin, Ramona Martinez and myself, I have located the sacred places where a quest for the matrilineal grants deeper access to feminine knowledge and ways of being. Taking up the cartographer's impulse has affirmed my will and my need to write within a context of healing. I am reminded that when we "ground" our identities in women's "histor[ies] of resistance," we are connected to a wellspring of feminine empowerment to transform our own and each other's lives (Anzaldúa 43). Ultimately, a search for the matrilineal is an inquiry to love all parts of ourselves. It is a yearning to be in closer proximity to the feminine imagination and to the inner mother, as we acquire our own psychological and creative strategies, the kind that present us with a greater capacity to live more authentically in our lives.

Notes

1 To symbolize this "marriage," Pippa wore a white wedding dress that was specifically designed for this expedition.
2 Pippa planned to travel through the Balkans on her way to her final destination, Jerusalem. She made it as far as Turkey. Twelve days into her journey, she was raped and murdered outside of Istanbul.

References

Anzaldúa, Gloria. *Borderlands/La Frontera: The New Mestiza*. San Francisco. Aunt Lute Books. 1999.
Léger, Natalie. *The White Dress*. London. Les Fugitives. 2020.

Index

For Product Safety Concerns and Information please contact our EU
representative GPSR@taylorandfrancis.com
Taylor & Francis Verlag GmbH, Kaufingerstraße 24, 80331 München, Germany